Chelsea House
An imprint of Infobase Publishing
132 West 31st Street
New York, NY 10001

Library of Congress Cataloging-in-Publication Data

Peoples and cultures of Africa / edited by Peter Mitchell.
    p. cm.
    "Authors, Amy-Jane Beer ... [et al.]"—T.p. verso.
    Includes bibliographical references and index.

    Set ISBN 0-8160-6260-9 (acid-free paper)

Nations & Personalities of Africa ISBN 0-8160-6266-8
Peoples and Cultures of Southern Africa ISBN 0-8160-6265-X
Peoples and Cultures of Central Africa ISBN 0-8160-6264-1
Peoples and Cultures of East Africa ISBN 0-8160-6263-3
Peoples and Cultures of West Africa ISBN 0-8160-6262-5
Peoples and Cultures of North Africa ISBN 0-8160-6261-7

    1. Africa—Civilization. 2. Ethnology—Africa. I. Beer, Amy-Jane. II. Mitchell, Peter, 1962-
    DT14.P46 2006
    960—dc22
                                    2006040011

Printed and bound in China

10 9 8 7 6 5 4 3 2 1

For The Brown Reference Group plc.
Project Editor: Graham Bateman
Editors: Peter Lewis, Virginia Carter
Cartographers: Darren Awuah, Mark Walker
Designers: Steve McCurdy, Martin Anderson
Managing Editor: Bridget Giles
Production Director: Alastair Gourlay
Editorial Director: Lindsey Lowe

Consultant Editor
Dr. Peter Mitchell is University Lecturer in African Prehistory, and holds a Tutorial Fellowship in Archaeology at St. Hugh's College, University of Oxford, United Kingdom. He is also Curator of African Archaeology at the Pitt Rivers Museum, Oxford, and an academic member of the multidisciplinary African Studies Centre based at St. Antony's College, Oxford. He has previously worked at the University of Cape Town. He serves on the Governing Council of the British Institute in Eastern Africa and is a member of the editorial boards of numerous journals. From 2004–2006 he held the post of President of the Society of Africanist Archaeologists.

Advisory Editor
Dr. David Johnson is University Lecturer in Comparative and International Education (Developing Countries) and a Fellow of St. Antony's College, University of Oxford, United Kingdom. He is a member of the African Studies Centre, based at St. Antony's College, and has conducted research into education in a wide range of African countries. He serves on the United Kingdom National Commission for UNESCO's working committee on Africa and on the editorial boards of two international journals.

Authors
Darryl Wilkinson
with
Amy-Jane Beer

Title page *The Virunga Mountains in the Democratic Republic of the Congo.*

CONTENTS

Peoples and Cultures of Africa provides a region-based study of Africa's main ethnic groups, cultures, languages, religions, music, and much more. Five of the six volumes cover large geographical regions, namely: *North Africa, West Africa, East Africa, Central Africa,* and *Southern Africa*. Each of these volumes starts with a series of overview articles covering the political situation today, physical geography, biomes, peoples, cultures, and finally a historical time line. The main articles that follow are arranged A–Z with four types of articles, each distinguished by a characteristic running-head logo and color panel:

ETHNIC GROUPS, such as Maasai, Zulu, Yoruba. Each ethnic group article includes a Fact File and a map, giving the approximate area in which a people mainly live.

MATERIAL CULTURE, such as Contemporary Art, Metalwork, Sculpture, Textiles

PERFORMING ARTS AND LITERATURE, such as African-language Literature, Masks and Masquerade, Dance and Song

RELIGION, SOCIETY, AND CULTURE, such as Islam, Christianity, Marriage and the Family

The sixth volume (*Nations and Personalities*) is divided into three main sections: *Political and Physical Africa* presents a complete overview of Africa, followed by profiles of every nation on the continent; *International Organizations* and *Environmental Organizations* review major international bodies operating in the region; and *African Personalities* gives biographies of some 300 people from throughout Africa.

Within each volume there is a *Glossary* of key terms, lists of *Further Resources* such as other reference books, and useful Web sites. Volume *Indexes* are provided in volumes 1–5, with a complete *Set Index* in volume 6.

CENTRAL AFRICA'S NATURAL RESOURCES ARE IMMENSE. HOWEVER, WARS AND POLITICAL UPHEAVAL HAVE CAUSED GREAT ECONOMIC DAMAGE TO THE REGION AND DETERRED INVESTORS; TWO OF AFRICA'S LONGEST-RUNNING CONFLICTS, IN ANGOLA AND THE DEMOCRATIC REPUBLIC OF THE CONGO, ONLY ENDED IN THE EARLY 2000s. YET THERE ARE PROMISING SIGNS OF GREATER STABILITY.

POPULATION AND ECONOMIC TRENDS

Central Africa has seen major population growth in the 20th and early 21st centuries. This growth has resulted from improvements in public sanitation and the introduction of modern medical treatments. Since the 1980s this trend has accelerated, with average annual population growth rates often exceeding 2.5 percent. This increase goes hand in hand with a rise in urbanization. Some 40 percent of the population of present-day Central Africa now live in cities. The main urban centers have grown up around the region's administrative capitals, principal mining areas, and seaports, where hopes of greater employment opportunities prompt large numbers of people to abandon rural ways of life. These hopes are often not realized and many city-dwellers in places such as Brazzaville and Kinshasa end up living in extreme poverty in makeshift shantytowns. Their living conditions are in stark contrast to those of the educated and wealthy urban elites, who inhabit large villas with stately gardens and high walls. As is the case with much of sub-Saharan Africa, the HIV/AIDS pandemic affects millions of Central Africans, especially in Zambia, where 8.2 percent of the adult population is infected.

Several countries in Central Africa have large mineral resources; this is an opencast manganese mine in Gabon. However, mineral wealth has sometimes not been fully exploited, or has been misused. For example, illegal diamond mining helped fund the longrunning civil war in Angola.

The two Congo republics, Zambia, and Gabon rely on mineral exports such as uranium, petroleum, and copper, while Cameroon, the Central African Republic, and Angola depend upon commercial agriculture, their main export crops being cotton, coffee, cacao, sugarcane, and tobacco. Oil exploration and export are vital to Angola's economy but were seriously disrupted for the duration of the civil war. The economic fortunes of each country vary widely, with some, such as Gabon and Cameroon, having relatively high living standards compared to the rest of Africa.

TURMOIL AND RECOVERY

Since independence most Central African states have had a turbulent history. All nations have been subject to one-party rule by repressive governments. Some regimes, such as that of Jean-Bedel Bokassa in the Central African Republic were as extravagant as they were violent. Bokassa crowned himself emperor in a lavish public ceremony in 1977 before he was overthrown two years later. However, since the 1990s democracy has been reinforced and many Central African states have instituted multiparty politics, including Gabon (1990), the Republic of Congo (1991), São Tomé and Príncipe (1991), Zambia (1991), Cameroon (1992), and the Central African Republic (1993).

The Democratic Republic of the Congo suffered under the corrupt Mobutu regime from 1965 until 1997, for much of which

time the country was called Zaïre. In 1996 a civil war broke out and a new government seized power under Laurent Kabila the following year. Since then, the renamed Democratic Republic of the Congo has suffered from ongoing ethnic tensions, political repression, and a breakdown of law and order in many areas. The neighboring country of Angola has also endured great turmoil, with a civil war ensuing after independence from Portugal was granted in 1975 between Marxist forces and pro-Western guerrillas. This conflict only finally ended in 2002, when a peace agreement was accepted by the the two warring factions.

A political map of Central Africa. The region is dominated by the huge Democratic Republic of the Congo (DRC). Instability grew when Hutu refugees from the genocides in Rwanda and Burundi crossed the border into DRC. Many Southern and East African countries were drawn into the DRC conflict.

VAST TROPICAL RAINFORESTS
DOMINATE CENTRAL AFRICA'S
LANDSCAPE, AND PLAYED A KEY
ROLE IN EUROPEANS' IMAGE OF
AFRICA AS THE "DARK CONTINENT."
YET THE LUSH, HUMID HABITAT
OF THE CONGO BASIN IS HOME
TO MANY PEOPLES AND IS RICH
IN WILDLIFE. ELSEWHERE IN
THE REGION, THE LANDSCAPE IS
CHARACTERIZED BY SAVANNA
AND MOUNTAINS.

THE CONGO BASIN

Every second the Congo (Zaïre) River
discharges some 1.2 million cubic feet
(34,000 cu m) of water into the Atlantic, a
volume exceeded only by the Amazon. The
Congo River follows a meandering course
to the sea from deep in the interior of Africa,
traveling first east and then south. It is
joined on its course by many tributaries,
and drains an area of more than 1.3 million
square miles (3.5 million sq km). The central
portion of the Congo is easily navigable, but
its western course passes through the low
mountain range that separates the basin
from the coast and has many fierce rapids,
making it less passable to boats. The courses
of the Congo and Ubangi make up the
greater part of the border between the
two Congo republics.

The wet climate of the Congo Basin,
which receives an average of 90 inches
(2,286 mm) of rainfall each year, supports
around 400,000 square miles (1 million sq
km) of tropical rainforest. Although atlases
often depict the equatorial belt as a solid
mass of trees, in reality the rainforest
consists of many different environments,
such as permanently dry forest, forest that
floods annually, and patchwork areas of
forest interspersed with savanna.

The central Congo Basin is where the Congo, Ubangi, and Sangha rivers converge, resulting in large areas of swampland and two major lakes, Mai-Ndombe and Tumba.

The Central African rainforest is sometimes referred to as a "jungle," a word that calls to mind a vast and forbidding mass of foliage, plagues of insects, and unknown perils. This term is misleading, since it characterizes the forested areas from the perspective of Europeans and not its indigenous inhabitants, for whom it provides ready shelter and plentiful food.

PLATEAUS AND GRASSLANDS

To the north and south of the Congo Basin, the forested areas gradually give way to less low-lying and more open savanna country. In the north, grasslands, criss-crossed by rivers, stretch from Cameroon to the Central African Republic and southern Sudan. In the south the elevations are somewhat higher, particularly the Bié Plateau, which makes up a sizable portion of Central Angola and the highlands of northern Zambia, where the Zambezi River rises.

The southern plateaus also include large areas of forest intermixed with the savanna. In the past the equatorial rainforest was far more extensive and would have covered much of what is now part of the savanna belt. Human activity is largely responsible for the extension of the grasslands, which have been maintained by using shifting cultivation methods.

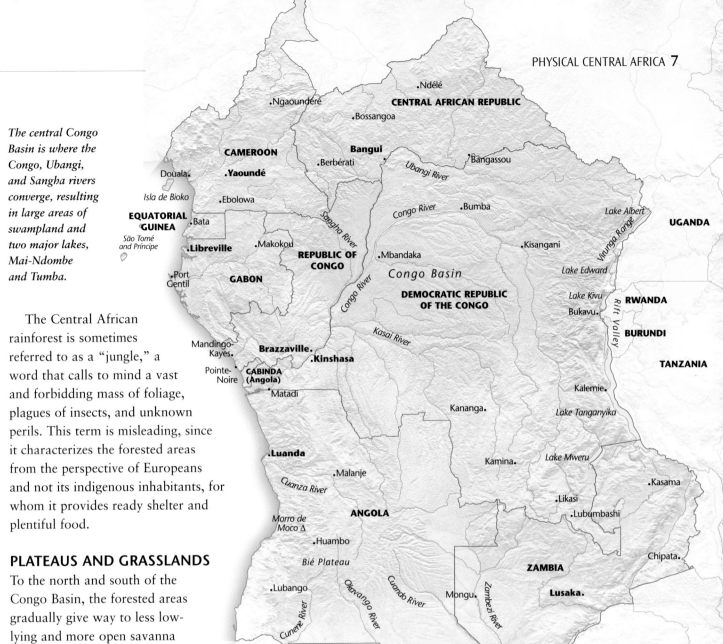

MOUNTAINS

The eastern edges of Central Africa are by far the most mountainous, where the Congo Basin gives way to the peaks of the western Great Rift Valley and the East African Great Lakes. North of Lake Kivu, running east–west from the edges of the Congo Basin to the Rift is the Virunga Mountains range. This area includes several active volcanoes, with major eruptions occurring in 1938, 1948, and 2002. The highest peak is Mt. Karisimbi, at 14,786 feet (4,507 m). A large part of the region forms the Virunga National Park, with its protected forests and wildlife species, including the mountain gorilla.

Map showing the main physical features of Central Africa. The mighty Congo River is the second longest in Africa after the Nile, with a total course of 2,716 miles (4,371 km).

CENTRAL AFRICA STRADDLES THE EQUATOR, STRETCHING AS FAR SOUTH AS THE TROPIC OF CAPRICORN. IT LIES ENTIRELY IN THE TROPICS, BUT THE CLIMATE IN THE SOUTH IS FAR MORE SEASONAL THAN THE NORTH, WITH DISTINCT WET AND DRY PERIODS AND GREATER VARIATION IN AVERAGE TEMPERATURE. IT HAS FOUR DISTINCT TYPES OF ECOSYSTEM.

TROPICAL MOIST BROADLEAF FOREST: THE CONGO BASIN

The Congo Basin is a vast geological depression, about 1.3 million square miles (3.5 million sq km) in area. Its average daytime temperatures range between 70 and 80°F (21–27°C) all year round. Humidity rarely drops below 80 percent and rainfall is frequent at all times of year, peaking in the spring and fall. Much of this eventually finds its way into the great Congo River. The Central African rainforest boasts up to 2,000 species of plants, of which some 10 percent are endemic to the region—that is, they are found nowhere else. This makes the Congo Basin, some parts of which are still largely unexplored, one of the richest areas of biodiversity in the world. Indeed, several quite large mammal species remained undiscovered until relatively recently—the okapi was not described until 1901, and the bonobo (or pygmy chimpanzee) and forest elephant were only recognized as species in their own right in 1929 and 2001 respectively.

TROPICAL GRASSLAND/SAVANNA: THE CENTRAL AFRICAN PLAIN

Much of Zambia and Angola and the southern half of the Democratic Republic of the Congo comprise flat plains dominated by dry savanna grassland and low scrub. Trees

are few and far between, thanks to regular fires. The rains are more seasonal here than farther north, with a marked wet season from November to April, followed by a cool dry period from May to July. August to October are hot and dry, and widespread drought prompts the migration of vast herds of grazing mammals including a herd of 30,000 blue wildebeest, which cross the border from Zambia to Angola in June and return in November with the rains.

MONTANE GRASSLAND

The highlands of western Angola are a patchwork of savanna and forest with a very different character to that of surrounding lowlands. The grasslands are maintained by regular burning, and the forests are restricted to steep, sheltered valleys and ravines. The highest point is Morro de Môco, at 8,596 ft (2,620 m). Altitude brings cooler temperatures than in the surrounding lowlands and rain is frequent in summer. In summer dense sea mists provide some moisture and help keep temperatures low. Civil war raged in Angola for 28 years (1975–2003), and the large animal population has been devastated by hunting for so-called bushmeat. The 360 or so native bird species may have fared better, although

Animal species of Central Africa:
1 *Demidoff's bush baby* (Galagoides demidoff);
2 *Okapi* (Okapia johnstoni); 3 *Bonobo* (Pan paniscus);
4 *Mandrill* (Mandrillus sphinx).

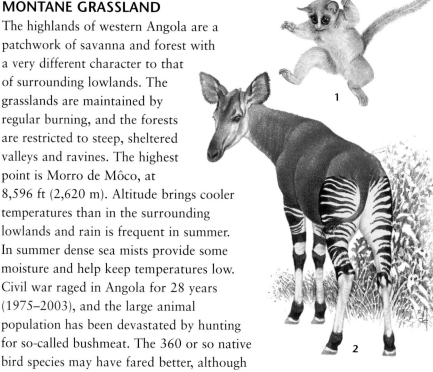

(Left) Huge herds of wildebeest undertake an annual migration in Central Africa in search of fresh grazing lands.

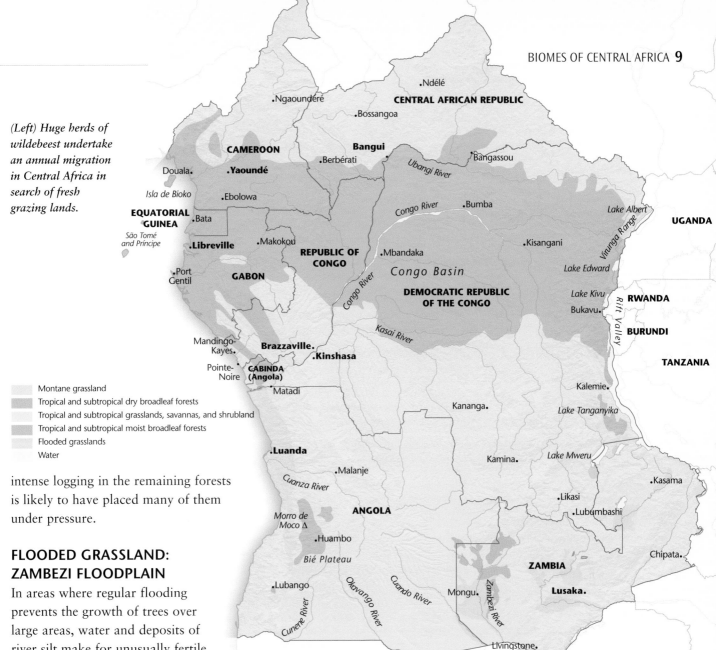

Montane grassland
Tropical and subtropical dry broadleaf forests
Tropical and subtropical grasslands, savannas, and shrubland
Tropical and subtropical moist broadleaf forests
Flooded grasslands
Water

intense logging in the remaining forests is likely to have placed many of them under pressure.

FLOODED GRASSLAND: ZAMBEZI FLOODPLAIN

In areas where regular flooding prevents the growth of trees over large areas, water and deposits of river silt make for unusually fertile soils. The largest areas are formed by the Zambezi and its tributaries, but pockets of similar habitat exist in scattered patches right across the central African plain. They form a marked contrast with the drier, less productive savannas that lie in between. The areas are hotspots for wildlife, supporting high densities of wetland birds, and large herds of grazing mammals and their predators.

TROPICAL DRY BROADLEAF FOREST: ZAMBEZIAN MAVUNDA

The dry forests of southern Zambia around the Kabompo River basin are composed chiefly of evergreen *mukwe* trees, with an understory of thicket vegetation draped in abundant lichen. The forests are dry; their quick-draining, sandy soils mean that no surface water builds up. Bird species include the crested guineafowl, several species of shrike, and the white-chested tinkerbird. The forests are also home to the blue and yellow-backed duiker, bushpig, African wild dogs, and elephants. The region's inaccessibility has helped it remain relatively undeveloped.

CENTRAL AFRICA HAS A REMARKABLY DIVERSE MOSAIC OF ETHNIC GROUPS. THE MODERN STATES IN THE REGION WERE CREATIONS OF COLONIALISM. AS A RESULT, THE CURRENT NATIONAL FRONTIERS TAKE NO ACCOUNT OF DIFFERENT ETHNIC AND LINGUISTIC AREAS. THE FANG, FOR EXAMPLE, LIVE IN CAMEROON, EQUATORIAL GUINEA, AND GABON, WHILE THE LUNDA PEOPLES LIVE IN THE DEMOCRATIC REPUBLIC OF THE CONGO AND ANGOLA.

The two most significant periods in the history of the peoples of Central Africa were the Bantu migrations and the rise of European colonialism. The Bantu-speaking peoples migrated into the Congo Basin during the 1st millennium B.C.E. and the first half of the 1st millennium C.E. and seem to have displaced many of the earlier populations of the region, such as the Mbuti. The beginning of European influence came with the arrival in the late 1400s of the Portuguese, who established trading links with the Kingdom of Kongo. European languages and religions were firmly established across Central Africa during the colonial era, and remain important today.

RELIGION
There are two main forms of religion in Central Africa: Christianity and preexisting beliefs. In theory a majority of its population are followers of Christianity, although in reality many are Christian in name only. Religious practices reflect a mixture of Christian and indigenous influences. Roman Catholicism is the main Christian denomination, particularly in the former

French, Belgian, and Portuguese colonies. These include Angola, Gabon, Rwanda, the Republic of Congo, and the Democratic Republic of Congo. Several Protestant churches also have large numbers of followers in most countries, and are predominant in the former British colony of Zambia. Central Africa has also given rise to its home-grown "charismatic" Christian sects. Notable among these is the Kimbanguist Church, which was founded in 1921. Today it has some 4 million members in the Democratic Republic of the Congo, making it Africa's largest independent church.

The preexisting religions of Central Africa are extremely diverse. In general, they center on the worship of ancestral spirits and nature spirits. A belief in the evil influence of witchcraft is also widespread among Central African peoples.

Below and opposite: Summary family trees of the Niger-Congo and Nilo-Saharan language groups. The ethnic groups featured in this volume are listed in parentheses after the relevant language.

NIGER-CONGO LANGUAGE FAMILY

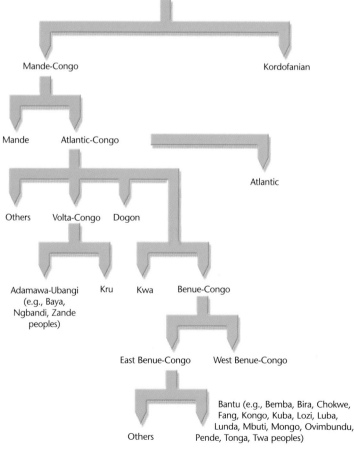

Mande-Congo

Kordofanian

Mande

Atlantic-Congo

Atlantic

Others

Volta-Congo

Dogon

Adamawa-Ubangi (e.g., Baya, Ngbandi, Zande peoples)

Kru

Kwa

Benue-Congo

East Benue-Congo

West Benue-Congo

Others

Bantu (e.g., Bemba, Bira, Chokwe, Fang, Kongo, Kuba, Lozi, Luba, Lunda, Mbuti, Mongo, Ovimbundu, Pende, Tonga, Twa peoples)

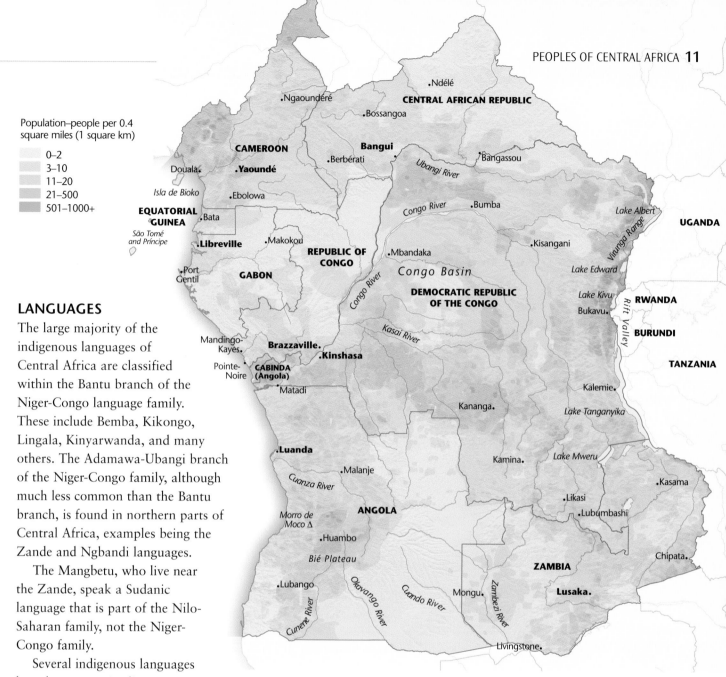

Population–people per 0.4
square miles (1 square km)

- 0–2
- 3–10
- 11–20
- 21–500
- 501–1000+

LANGUAGES

The large majority of the indigenous languages of Central Africa are classified within the Bantu branch of the Niger-Congo language family. These include Bemba, Kikongo, Lingala, Kinyarwanda, and many others. The Adamawa-Ubangi branch of the Niger-Congo family, although much less common than the Bantu branch, is found in northern parts of Central Africa, examples being the Zande and Ngbandi languages.

The Mangbetu, who live near the Zande, speak a Sudanic language that is part of the Nilo-Saharan family, not the Niger-Congo family.

Several indigenous languages have become major linguae francae—languages used by many nonnative speakers as common languages for trade—

Map showing the distribution of the population in Central Africa. The mouth of the Congo River and the areas west of the Rift Valley lakes in the east of the region show high population densities.

throughout Central Africa. Many of these languages have borrowed elements of vocabulary from European languages. Lingala, which became a major trading language throughout the Congo Basin during the 19th and 20th centuries, is an example of a Central African lingua franca.

Indo-European languages are widely spoken across Central Africa as a result of colonialism, the most prominent being English, Portuguese, and French. European languages are generally concentrated among the more urban and wealthy populations, and tend to dominate in the press, broadcast media, and government administration.

NILO-SAHARAN LANGUAGE FAMILY

- Songhai
- Saharan
- Others
  - East Sudanic
    - Surmic-Nilotic
    - Nubian
  - Others
  - Central Sudanic
    - Bongo
    - Mangbetu (e.g., Mangbetu, Mbenga peoples)
  - Fur

THE CULTURES OF CENTRAL AFRICA RANGE FROM THE RAINFOREST HUNTER-GATHERER SOCIETY OF THE MBUTI TO THE SETTLED FARMING COMMUNITIES OF THE TONGA ON THE DRY BUTONGA PLATEAU OF ZAMBIA. ACROSS THE REGION, THERE EXIST DYNAMIC TRADITIONS OF ORAL LITERATURE, MUSIC, SCULPTURE AND CRAFTS. CENTRAL AFRICA HAS A RICH AND VARIED HISTORY OF KINGDOMS AND VILLAGE-BASED SOCIETIES THAT WERE THRIVING LONG BEFORE THE RISE OF CITIES AND STATES IN THE COLONIAL AND POSTCOLONIAL ERAS.

ARTS AND CRAFTS

Central Africa has a long and highly developed tradition of material art forms. These are represented in Western museums, galleries, and collections primarily by wooden sculptures and masks, and to a lesser extent by textiles. There is a wide range of regional styles, from the masks of the Chokwe to the royal portrait figures of the Kuba, reflecting the cultures that produced them as well as the artistic abilities of the individual sculptors. For most Central African peoples such objects have important ritual functions and symbolism beyond their simple role as art objects.

Metals and stone are less common in Central African arts, but by no means unknown. Copper, brass, and iron were often used to make not just tools, but also prestigious objects to form part of royal regalia, since control over mining and trading metals represented kingly authority and power. Contemporary artists from the region, such as Leandro Nsue (b.1938) from Equatorial Guinea and Trigo Piula (b.1950) from the Republic of Congo are noted for the inspiration they draw from older art forms when creating, respectively, their modern sculptures and paintings.

MUSIC AND DANCE

Various forms of musical instrument are found among Central African peoples, including harps, flutes, trumpets, drums, xylophones, and lamellaphones. Music and dance are an integral part of ceremonial functions, funerary rites, initiations and religious rituals, as well as being performed just for entertainment. The Mbuti people of the remote Ituri forest in the northwestern Democratic Republic of the Congo have become well known for their polyphonic singing. In the 20th and 21st centuries, many musicians from the region have enthusiastically adopted modern instruments

BUBI

The Bubi inhabit the island of Bioko, now part of Equatorial Guinea, where they form a majority of the population. Their ancestors came to the island from the African mainland from c.1200 on. There, they developed largely in isolation, abandoning ironworking for lack of local sources of the metal. When the Portuguese came to the island in the late 15th century, the Bubi successfully resisted colonization. Bioko remained independent until 1858, when it came under Spanish control. During the colonial period large numbers of Fang settlers were brought to Bioko by the Spanish as plantation workers. Equatorial Guinea, which comprises a mainland region (once known as Río Muni) and Bioko, gained its independence in 1968. Since then, the Fang have dominated the country's government. The Bubi, who make up only 15 percent of the country's entire population, have been subject to repression, especially since a failed uprising in 1998.

A Mangbetu woman holding her baby. The child's head is bound with rope to elongate its skull, a feature that is considered attractive among this people.

dancing, creating an event in which the audience are encouraged to participate alongside the performers.

The early stages in the development of the written literature of the region were strongly influenced by oral literatures, and more recent writers, such as the Malawian Steve Chimombo (b.1945), who writes chiefly about Zambia, continue to be inspired by oral traditions. The principal themes in Central African written literature include the ravages of the colonial regime, the influence of modern, capitalist culture, and the clash between modern and pre-colonial attitudes toward religion, the family, and the role of women. French is the main language in which Central African authors write, although Portuguese and English are also of importance.

A Mangbetu jar for storing palm wine. Many objects made by this people, including harps and trumpets, feature realistic miniature sculptures of human heads.

such as the electric guitar, with homegrown styles such as the Congolese rumba (or soukous) proving enormously popular across sub-Saharan Africa and even achieving international recognition.

WRITTEN AND ORAL LITERATURES

Oral literature was the way in which Central African societies passed on the history of their people and culture before the rise of colonialism and the arrival of written literature. Storytelling still forms a key part of social life in the region. It is often accompanied by music, performing, and

MANGBETU

Specifically referring to the aristocracy who once ruled over the people of the northern Democratic Republic of the Congo, the term *Mangbetu* is now applied to the people of that region as a whole. Mangbetu ruling lineages entered this area from Sudan in the 19th century, intermarrying with and dominating its original Bantu-speaking and Mbuti inhabitants. They remained a major political force until the arrival of Arab slavers, and later on the Belgian colonial authorities, from 1880 on. Mixed farming and trade form the basis of their economy. The Mangbetu developed a distinctive woodcarving style, making elaborate sculptures, musical instruments, and thrones. Mangbetu art changed greatly in the 20th century, in part because of the new markets that developed for it in the West.

2.5 million years ago The hominid *Homo rudolfensis* is living in East Central Africa and using stone tools.

200,000 years ago Humans (*Homo sapiens*) are living at Kabwe in East Central Africa (Zambia). Stone tools of a type known as Sangoan are in use in Central Africa.

40,000 years ago Microlithic stone tool industries begin to appear in Central Africa.

2400 B.C.E. Ancient Egyptian texts refer to the rainforest inhabitants (ancestors of the Mbuti, Twa, and Mbenga) of Central Africa.

c.400 B.C.E. Ironworking is practiced in the northwest of Central Africa (modern Cameroon and Gabon). Bananas, an Indonesian crop by origin, may already be being cultivated by this time in Cameroon. The expansion of Bantu-speaking farming peoples from an original homeland in Cameroon is underway.

c.100 C.E. Bantu-speaking farming peoples are now intensively settling much of the Congo Basin. Around this time, Adamawa-Ubangi speaking peoples migrate into northern Central Africa.

c.650 Bantu-speaking peoples are established over much of Central Africa by this time.

c.1000 Greater long-distance trade, mostly by river, takes place in Central Africa, leading to several centralized chiefdoms developing within the region. Archaeological excavations in the Upemba Depression of the Katanga region of the Democratic Republic of the Congo suggest connections with the later Luba state. Banana cultivation is widespread among farmers living in the more heavily forested regions of Central Africa.

1300–1400 Emergence of the kingdom of Kongo on the lower reaches of the Congo River. The Ndongo kingdom appears farther to the south around the same time.

1470 Portuguese explorers first land on the Gabonese coast.

1471 The Portuguese first chart the island of Fernando Póo (modern Bioko in Equatorial Guinea).

1477 Spain claims control of Fernando Póo.

1483 The Portuguese navigator Diogo Cão explores the mouth of the Congo River and establishes contact with the kingdom of Kongo.

1491 Official conversion of the king and court of Kongo to Christianity.

1520 The Portuguese encounter the Ndongo kingdom in northern Angola. Although they were after other commodities at first, the Portuguese begin to develop the slave trade in Central Africa. The island of São Tomé is the main exporting depot. Some three million slaves are thought to have been shipped from Central Africa to the Americas before the slave trade is finally brought to a close in the late 19th century.

1545 Death of Afonso I, the first Christian *mani kongo* (ruler) of the kingdom of Kongo.

1550 The Luba kingdom arises in the southeast of what is now the Democratic Republic of the Congo (DRC).

1568 The Jaga invasions of the kingdom of Kongo take place.

1571 Paulo Dias de Novais is granted a charter to found a Portuguese colony at Luanda Bay, Angola. The Portuguese successfully repel the Jaga invaders from the kingdom of Kongo.

1576 The Portuguese port of Luanda is founded, becoming a major link in the transatlantic slave trade and the center of the colony of Angola.

1596 Mbanza Kongo, the Kongo capital, is rebuilt in stone and made a Roman Catholic bishopric.

Fernando Póo in the Gulf of Guinea was inhabited by the Bubi, a Bantu people, when the Portuguese first landed on the island in the 1470s. Now renamed Bioko, it is part of the state of Equatorial Guinea; descendants of the Bubi still live there.

c.1600 Kuba kingdom develops in the center of what is now the DRC. Trade increases in ivory, collected by peoples of the Central African interior and passed on via middlemen to Europeans on the coast. The Chokwe split from the Lunda and found a separate kingdom in northern Angola.

1641 A Dutch–Ndongo alliance succeeds in taking Luanda and the surrounding region from Portugal.

1648 The Portuguese regain control of Luanda and their Angolan colony.

1650 The Bembe state emerges in the Central Highlands of Angola. The Bemba kingdom emerges in what is now Zambia.

1660 The slave trade reaches new heights, with people becoming the largest single "commodity" exported from Central Africa.

1665 The Portuguese successfully conquer the kingdom of Kongo at the Battle of Ambuila, beating the Kongo–Dutch alliance.

c.1700 Emergence of the Lunda empire in what is now the south of the Democratic Republic of the Congo.

c.1750 Zande principalities arise in northeastern Central Africa.

Belgian king Leopold II (1865–1909) established his personal and tyrannical rule over the Congo Free State (the present-day DRC) in 1885.

c.1800 The Ovimbundu kingdom develops in what is now Angola. The Lozi kingdom is now the most important state in western Zambia, while the Kazembe kingdom controls much of northern Zambia.

1844 The Spanish establish a colony in the coastal enclave of Río Muni (now the mainland part of Equatorial Guinea).

1850s Muslim traders from the East African coast conduct slave raids on Central African peoples such as the Luba.

1852–73 British missionary David Livingstone explores large parts of Central Africa. His efforts to bring Christianity and end slavery open up the interior to European colonization at the end of the 19th century. The transatlantic slave trade begins to decline.

1870s King Leopold II of the Belgians invests his own capital in exploring the area of the Congo Basin.

1874 British–U.S. explorer Henry Morton Stanley charts the Congo River on behalf of Leopold II.

Henry Morton Stanley (1841–1904) met David Livingstone at Ujiji on Lake Tanganyika in 1871, greeting him with the famous words "Dr. Livingstone, I presume?"

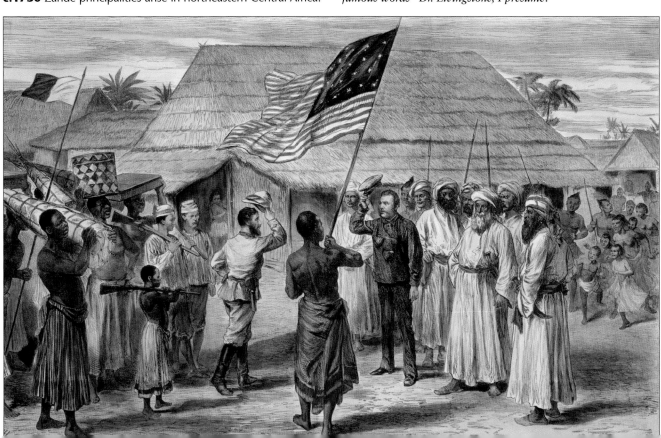

1880s The Lunda empire begins to break up, as the Chokwe invade Lunda territory and take control of the court.

1884 The German empire colonizes Cameroon. Chancellor Bernard von Bülow refers to his country's entry into the colonial race as claiming its rightful "place in the sun."

1884–85 At the Berlin Conference on Africa, European powers divide up the continent. Leopold II's private colony in the Central African interior is recognized as the Congo Free State. The expanding Chokwe kingdom of northern Angola and southern Congo (Kinshasa) conquers several neighboring peoples.

1886 Zanzibari slavers from the East African coastal region begin raiding Zandeland.

1890 The Barotseland Treaty delivers the Lozi kingdom to the British South Africa Company as part of the protectorate of Northern Rhodesia (now Zambia).

1892 The southern part (Katanga) of the Congo Free State falls under Leopold II's control. The Congo Free State experiences a boom in rubber tapping and trading, through forced labor of Congolese people.

A cartoon of 1906 shows Leopold II as a rubber-coiled snake squeezing the life out of an African. Outrage at cruelty in the Congo forced the Belgian state to take control of the colony in 1908.

1894 The French establish the colonial dependency of Ubangi-Shari in what is now the Central African Republic, after several decades of commercial activity in the region. By the end of the 19th century, most of the surviving indigenous kingdoms and peoples of Central Africa have been incorporated into the European colonies.

French and British forces invade the German colony of Kamerun in 1915, during World War I. In the "Scramble for Africa," Germany had secured Cameroon as a protectorate in 1884.

1902–03 The Ovimbundu wage the Bailundo War against Portuguese colonization of Angola.

1908 International condemnation of the brutal treatment of the peoples of the Congo Free State forces the Belgian government to take control; the territory is renamed the Belgian Congo.

1910 Ubangi-Shari and Gabon are formally incorporated into French Equatorial Africa. Collapse of the Congo Free State rubber trade.

1915–16 French and British forces seize Cameroon from the Germans during World War I.

1919 Cameroon is divided into British and French territories under a mandate from the League of Nations, with most of the colony (around 80 percent) falling within the French zone.

1924 The Congo–Ocean railroad is completed by the French, using forced labor. It links the interior of French Equatorial Africa to the Atlantic coastline.

1920s–1930s A diamond rush begins in the Congo (the present-day DRC) and exploitation of the Zambian copperbelt begins. Large numbers of African people move to the towns and industrial areas to find work.

1939–40 African mineworkers strike in Northern Rhodesia.

1951 Angola is reclassified as an overseas province of Portugal, rather than a colony, although little practical change is evident in the lives of its African majority.

1953 Northern Rhodesia (Zambia), Southern Rhodesia (Zimbabwe), and Nyasaland (Malawi) are amalgamated into a federation dominated by the white settler government of Southern Rhodesia.

1956 Formation of the Movimento Popular de Libertaçao de Angola (MPLA; "Popular Movement for the Liberation of Angola").

1957 Oil is struck in the Republic of Congo; it becomes a major part of the region's export economy in the later 20th century (notably in Gabon and, more recently, Equatorial Guinea and São Tomé and Principe).

1958 Construction of the Kariba Dam on the Zambezi River along the Zimbabwe–Zambia border is completed. Large areas are flooded, with many people being forced to abandon their homes and resettle.

1960 The Republic of Congo, the Central African Republic, Gabon, and French Cameroon win independence from France. Most of British Cameroon becomes part of Nigeria. Belgium grants the Belgian Congo independence under President Joseph Kasavubu. Katanga province tries to break away from the Congo, sparking a civil war. United Nations forces are deployed to try to halt the conflict, which becomes part of the wider Cold War between the West and the Soviet Union. Che Guevara leads a Cuban guerilla group supporting the Congolese government. U.N. Secretary-General Dag Hammarskjöld dies in a plane crash in Congo while trying to end the war (1961).

1962 The Central African Republic becomes a one-party state.

1963 The Federation of Rhodesia and Nyasaland is dissolved.

European refugees fleeing from the former Belgian Congo in 1960. Fighting between rival factions broke out almost immediately after Congo (Kinshasa) had won independence.

1964 Northern Rhodesia gains independence under President Kenneth Kaunda and is renamed Zambia. The Republic of Congo becomes a one-party socialist state under Massamba-Débat, leader of the National Revolutionary Movement.

1965 Jean-Bédel Bokassa overthrows President Dacko's government in a military coup in the Central African Republic (CAR). Colonel Joseph Mobutu comes to power in the Congo (now the DRC). Rebel forces in the Congolese Katanga copper region are defeated.

1966 Cameroon becomes a one-party state.

1968 A coup brings Marien Ngouabi, leader of the Congolese Workers' Party, to power in the Republic of Congo. Spanish Guinea achieves independence and is renamed Equatorial Guinea under President Francisco Maçias Nguema. A one-party state is created in Gabon.

1971 President Joseph Mobutu renames the Congo Zaïre. As part of a program to assert "authentic" African culture, he declares that all citizens must have non-European names, himself becoming Mobutu Sese Seko.

1972 A one-party state is formed in Zambia under Kenneth Kaunda's United National Independence Party. Bokassa declares himself "president for life" in CAR.

1973 President Mobutu nationalizes major industries in Zaïre and closes the country to foreign investment.

1974 Revolution against Portuguese dictatorship leads Portugal to abandon its African colonies (Angola and Mozambique).

1975 Civil war erupts in Angola between the Marxist MPLA (backed by the Soviet Union and Cuba) and pro-Western UNITA and FNLA forces. South Africa intervenes in Angola in support of UNITA. TanZam railroad built (with Chinese aid), linking Zambian copperbelt to Tanzanian coast and reducing Zambian dependence on white-ruled Rhodesia.

1977 The Central African Republic is renamed the Central African Empire and its leader, Jean-Bédel Bokassa, crowns himself emperor in a lavish public ceremony.

1979 Agostinho Neto, founding president of Angola, dies and is succeeded by Jose Eduardo Dos Santos. Emperor Bokassa's regime is overthrown in the Central African Republic after many schoolchildren are slaughtered by government forces during public protests. Former President David Dacko is restored to power and the country's name reverts to the Central African Republic. The repressive President Nguema of Equatorial Guinea is deposed in a coup led by his nephew, Teodoro Obiang Nguema Mbasogo, who does not greatly improve human rights.

1981 A military coup, led by Andre Kolinga, ousts President Dacko in the Central African Republic.

1982 Paul Biya becomes president of Cameroon.

1983–84 Acute drought hits São Tomé and Príncipe.

1988 South African forces withdraw from Angola following an agreement that Cuban troops backing the MPLA government will also return home.

1990 Gabon becomes a multiparty democracy.

1991 The Lisbon peace treaty between UNITA and the governing MPLA is signed. President Mobutu makes some concessions to political opponents in Zaïre. Multiparty democracy is restored in Zambia and Frederick Chiluba is elected president.

1992 Multiparty democracy is restored (temporarily) in the Republic of Congo, the Central African Republic and (nominally) in Cameroon.

1993 Multiparty politics are permitted in Equatorial Guinea by the ruling regime but are widely seen as flawed.

1994 The Lusaka peace accord is signed by the MPLA government and UNITA, bringing a temporary end to Angola's civil war. The Rwandan genocide takes place, forcing hundreds of thousands of Hutu to flee over the border into Zaïre (the present-day DRC).

Angolan MPLA government forces being trained to fight against UNITA and FNLA rebels. Angola became a pawn in the Cold War, with the USSR and the USA funding rival groups for decades.

1995 An outbreak of the deadly Ebola virus kills 245 people around the town of Kikwit in Zaïre.

1996 President Obiang Nguema wins 99 percent of votes in Equatorial Guinea; elections widely seen as fraudulent.

1997 The Mobutu regime falls in Zaïre, with rebels helped by Tutsi forces from Rwanda. The country's name is changed to the Democratic Republic of the Congo (DRC). Laurent Kabila becomes president.

1998 An uprising takes place against Kabila's government in the DRC with aid from Rwanda and Uganda. Angola, Namibia, and Zimbabwe send military forces to support the government, but the rebels succeed in taking control of the eastern portion of the country. Civil war breaks out again in Angola.

1999 A peace accord is agreed in Lusaka between the DRC, Zimbabwe, Namibia, Uganda, Rwanda, and Angola. UN peacekeepers are sent to the region.

2001 Laurent Kabila, president of the DRC, is assassinated. He is replaced by his son Joseph Kabila.

Many Hutu refugees from the violence that broke out in Rwanda in 1994 fled across the border into Zaïre. This helped destabilize that country, which witnessed conflict up to 2002.

2002 A peace agreement is reached between the DRC and Rwanda, with Rwanda agreeing to withdraw troops from the eastern territories. Levy Mwanawasa becomes president of Zambia. Jonas Savimbi, leader of UNITA, is killed by Angolan government forces. UNITA and the MPLA sign a lasting cease-fire, ending the Angolan civil war.

2003 Military leader François Bozizé seizes power in the Central African Republic.

2004 Coup attempt by white mercenaries in Equatorial Guinea is foiled. HIV/AIDS is now a serious health problem across the region, made worse in many countries by decades of civil war.

2005 A new constitution is agreed for the Democratic Republic of the Congo. Marburg virus, more deadly than Ebola, kills 300 in northern Angola.

MAJOR WORKS AND THEIR AUTHORS

Title	Date	Author	Language
Kwenkwenda	1943	Emile Disengomoka	Kikongo
Kinkonzi ye ntekelo andi Makundu (Kinkonzi and his Grandson Makundu)	1948	Jacques N. Bahele	Kikongo
Mnyamboza (Headman's Enterprise)	1949	Samuel Yosia Ntara	Nyanja
Liswanelo za kuna kwa li lu sile (How Not to Treat Animals)	1954	M. M. Sakubila	Lozi
Uwakwensho bushiku (He Who Leads You Through the Night)	1955	Stephen Mpashi	Bemba
Kubuca ulela tunji (Everyday Brings Something New)	1956	M. C. Mainza	Tonga
Niklisto mu Kongo dia kimpwanza (The Christian in Independent Congo)	1965	Homère-Antoine Wantwadi	Kikongo

SINCE INDEPENDENCE, CENTRAL AFRICAN AUTHORS HAVE WRITTEN EXTENSIVELY IN FRENCH, ENGLISH, AND PORTUGUESE. ONLY A LIMITED AMOUNT OF LITERATURE FROM THIS REGION HAS APPEARED IN AFRICAN LANGUAGES.

The primary reason for the lack of Central African-language literature is that even those languages of the region that are widespread are spoken by relatively few people. Swahili from East Africa and Hausa from West Africa each have some 30–40 million speakers. By contrast, the largest languages of Central Africa are spoken by no more than 10 million people, and many Central African languages have only a few hundred thousand speakers. As a result, the markets for works written in African languages are extremely limited.

Second, low literacy levels in Central Africa, especially in rural areas, mean that many people do not read literature of any kind. Also, the more educated urban populations are far more likely to read works published in French or Portuguese than in an African language. This is due in part to the widespread notion that European languages carry greater prestige as a sign of a high level of education.

HISTORICAL DEVELOPMENT

The Bible was the first written work to appear in almost all of the region's languages. There were also several attempts in the 18th and 19th centuries to record oral tales and folklore in writing. In the early 20th century, members of the Kimbanguist Church composed hymns in Kikongo as an alternative to European hymns. Scholarly journals also appeared in order to promote African languages, such as *Echo de Angola*, which began in 1881 as a forum for Kimbundu poetry and fiction.

Writers in some Congolese languages, such as Tshiluba, produced poetic works as early as 1914, but it was not until the mid-20th century that novels began to appear. Today Tshiluba, Kikongo, and Lingala are the main literary languages of the two Congo republics. The monthly journal *La Voix du Congolais* helped promote African-language works. In Zambia, the Ministry of Education has published works in Bemba since the late 1960s.

Some individual authors actively promote literature in African languages such as Kiba-Mwenyu, a poet from Angola who writes in Kimbundu, Portuguese, and English. His Kimbundu works include the international award-winning poem *Ngundu-a-Ndala* ("Songbird"). Another such writer is Sony Labou Tansi (b.1947), who has written poems in Kikongo as well as several novels in French. It is often the case that poetry in African languages, being shorter in length, is more widely published than novels.

SEE ALSO: Christianity; English-language literature; French-language literature; Oral literature; Portuguese-language literature.

ARCHITECTURE

BUILDING TECHNIQUES

Material/ technique	Description
Adobe/Banco	Adobe bricks are made from blocks of sandy clay mixed with straw and/or animal dung that are allowed to dry out in the open air. Banco is a similar construction material made using sun-dried blocks composed of mixed clay and grain chaff.
Concrete	Concrete is a European introduction, a stonelike material made by mixing cement, water, gravel and sand that is allowed to harden. It is used in large urban buildings. Concrete blocks are used in many shantytown houses and also provide a flooring material in some regions.
Leaf stems	Flexible leaf stems, such as those of plants of the Olacaceae family, are sharpened at one end and inserted into the ground, with the stems bent to form a framework which is the basis of light dwellings such as domed Mbuti houses. The leaf stems are then covered with leaves to complete the structure.
Metal	The use of metal in buildings is a European introduction and is found on a large scale in the steel girders of modern office buildings. Galvanized tin is also used as a roofing material in many poorer urban dwellings.
Pau-à-pique	A type of wall construction using a latticework made from lengths of cane twisted into bundles. Reeds are woven between the cane bundles which are secured to the ground. This forms a dense mesh that is then covered in clay.
Raffia palm	Raffia palm is widely used for building by the Kuba; it is woven to form a textile, rectangular sections of which are used as panels in constructing walls.
Thatch	A roofing material in which many layers of straw or dried reeds are used to form a sloping covering.
Wattle-and-Daub	Wattle-and-daub is a building technique in which a framework of poles is inserted into the ground and covered with clay to form a wall.
Wood	Before the colonial period, stone buildings were virtually unknown in Central Africa, unsurprisingly given the lack of suitable building stone in Equatorial Africa. The abundant forests provided ample building materials, although actual timber was generally only found in the larger buildings and halls, used as supporting posts or carved to form ornamental door frames.

THE MAJOR KINGDOMS THAT EXISTED IN THIS REGION BEFORE THE ARRIVAL OF EUROPEANS PUT UP FEW LARGE PUBLIC BUILDINGS. RATHER, THE MOST TYPICAL CENTRAL AFRICAN ARCHITECTURE IS REPRESENTED BY THE HOMES OF ORDINARY PEOPLE. COLONIALISM HAD A HUGE IMPACT, CHANGING BOTH THE TYPES OF BUILDINGS THAT WERE CONSTRUCTED AND THE MATERIALS USED TO MAKE THEM.

PRECOLONIAL ARCHITECTURE

Reflecting the great diversity of Central African peoples and their habitats, most regional styles of building were localized and specific to their culture. A wide variety of different house shapes were—and still are—made, such as the roundhouses of the Zande and Mangbetu with their large conical roofs made of thatch, and the more rectangular houses of the Fang, with their pitched roofs. Rainforest peoples such as the Mbuti, Twa, and Mbenga are noted for their dome-shaped houses, made from a framework of leaf stems and roofed over with leaves, which allows smoke from the central fireplace to filter out. The Kuba house is rectangular, with its roof thatched using palm leaves and walls that are highly

In the Ituri Forest in the northeast of the Democratic Republic of the Congo, a Mbuti woman constructs a temporary, rounded leaf-stem shelter from pliable tree saplings.

decorated with colored textiles, especially if the occupant is a person of high social standing. The Kuba also built large palatial structures for the king to hold court in. These included the Nyimi complex at the Kuba capital of Mushenge, which boasted a main hall with a ceiling 18 feet (5.5 m) high, together with many other gabled buildings and courtyards. In areas of the Congo Basin that are criss-crossed by rivers and tributaries, many peoples, such as the Chokwe, Lunda, and Luba, live in houses that are adapted to cope with annual floods. These dwellings are set high on stilts and are reached by ramps leading up to their doors.

The colonial regimes that occupied Central Africa in the late 19th century made efforts to change local building practices. In particular, roundhouses were discouraged in favor of rectangular buildings, which were seen as more "civilized" because they looked more like European homes. The colonial authorities also regarded buildings without separate rooms as distasteful, and people who refused to comply with colonial standards could be severely punished. Today, with the exception of the Mbuti and related groups, many Central African people have abandoned their traditional forms of architecture, with colonial styles becoming firmly established even in rural areas.

HERBERT LANG AND KING OKONDO'S HALL

Between 1909 and 1915, Herbert Lang, a scholar from the American Museum of Natural History, led an expedition to the Mangbetu people of the eastern Congo Basin. Earlier descriptions of this culture from the 1870s included sketches showing King Mbunza's great audience hall, which was used for feasts and royal audiences. Yet by the time Lang arrived, this building had disappeared. Lang mentioned to his host, King Okondo, that he was disappointed to have missed seeing the great hall. Okondo promptly ordered that a new one be built, and when Lang returned the following year, he was amazed to see an enormous hall, 30 feet (9 m) high and 180 feet (55 m) long, supported by massive wooden pillars, some of which were carved with geometric designs.

COLONIAL ARCHITECTURE

The first colonial structures to appear in Africa were churches built by the Portuguese. These were constructed in the late 15th century in the areas where missionaries from Portugal had introduced Christianity, such as the kingdom of Kongo. As Portuguese involvement in Central Africa grew over the following centuries, particularly with the rise of the transatlantic slave trade, much larger and more impressive buildings appeared, such as the cathedral at Luanda, the capital of modern Angola, which was completed in 1628. This cathedral, which was built of stone and had large, square bell towers with domed summits and circular and arched windows, would have been an impressive sight in the 17th century. Like much colonial architecture, it was built to express the

(Left) New village housing in Angola. Colonial influence saw many people adopt rectangular structures as their building style. More recently, the traditional roundhouse form has been revived, but using modern materials.

power and authority of the European colonizers and their Christian faith. The Portuguese colonial style of Central Africa has many similarities to the architectural styles seen in contemporary Brazil, a reflection of the strong links between these areas via the transatlantic slave trade.

As European settlement and control of Central Africa increased in the late 19th and early 20th centuries, an international colonial style developed, creating buildings that looked very similar regardless of whether they were in areas run by the British, French, Germans, Belgians, or Portuguese. Based on Portuguese-influenced architecture, such houses commonly had two storys, each with a surrounding verandah or porch to create a free flow of air in the hot and humid equatorial climate. Government buildings in the colonial capitals were often extremely large and imposing, and were built of durable materials.

MODERN CENTRAL AFRICAN CITIES

Modern cities in Central Africa display a number of different styles of architecture. Kinshasa, for example, the capital of the Democratic Republic of the Congo, contains many buildings that were originally put up by the colonial regime and have since been adapted to serve as government buildings in the postindependence era. These buildings stand side-by-side with multistory office blocks in the business district, which were erected from the 1960s on and are made of concrete, steel, and glass. These skyscrapers are universal symbols of modern commerce. The modernist style was eagerly adopted in Central Africa (as elsewhere) as a deliberate rejection of the traditional, European-inspired architecture of the colonial period and the repressive and outmoded attitudes that such buildings represented.

Those who are too poor to live in colonial mansions or modern, spacious apartment blocks, such as migrant laborers and other disadvantaged sections of the community, live in shantytowns. Buildings in these makeshift settlements are made of banco, sheets of corrugated iron, or concrete blocks. The shantytowns serve as a reminder that the end of colonialism has not brought improvements for all sections of Central African society.

Modern office skyscrapers and apartment blocks characterize the center of the Angolan capital Luanda. Reminders of the colonial past in this port city include a 17th-century Portuguese fortress.

SEE ALSO: Chokwe; Christianity; Kuba; Luba; Lunda; Mbuti, Twa, and Mbenga.

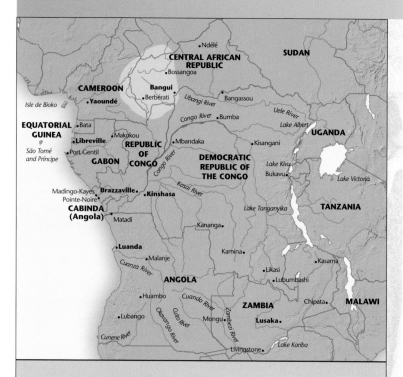

FACT FILE

Population	c.1.3 million Baya, mostly in Central African Republic
Religion	Baya religion; Christianity
Language	The Baya language is found in the Adamawa-Ubangi branch of the Niger-Congo language family. Many Baya speak Sango, another Adamawa-Ubangi tongue, which is the common language of the CAR.

TIMELINE

c.1000	The Baya settle in the Central African savanna.
1804–19	Rise of the Fulani Sokoto Caliphate in northern Nigeria.
c.1820	Fulani expansion forces Baya to migrate into the southwestern portion of the Central African Republic.
1894	The French colony of Ubangi-Shari is established.
1923–24	The French authorities build the Congo–Ocean railroad using forced Baya labor.
1928	Beginning of the Kongo Wara War, an anti-French uprising in which the Baya participated.
1931	The French crush the rebellion with much bloodshed.
1930s	The diamond rush begins with many Baya flocking to the mines to seek employment.
1960	The Central African Republic (CAR) wins independence.
1965–79	Rule of Jean-Bédel Bokassa in Central African Republic. Bokassa declares himself emperor with a lavish lifestyle.
1993	Multiparty politics introduced in the CAR.

THE BAYA (OR GBAYA) ARE SPREAD ACROSS SEVERAL PRESENT-DAY CENTRAL AFRICAN STATES, MAINLY INHABITING THE SOUTHWESTERN CENTRAL AFRICAN REPUBLIC (CAR), EASTERN AND CENTRAL CAMEROON, AND THE NORTHERN PARTS OF THE TWO CONGO REPUBLICS.

HISTORY

It is thought that the Baya first appeared in the northern savannas of Central Africa in the 10th century. They settled in their current location, farther south, in the early 19th century. Their migration was prompted by the expansion from northern Nigeria of the Sokoto Caliphate under the Fulani leader Usman dan Fodio. By the late 19th century the Baya had come under the influence of the colonial powers and in 1894 most were incorporated into Ubangi-Shari, a section of French Equatorial Africa. The French imposed a harsh regime on the Baya, including forced labor on the railroads, which cost many lives.

In the late 1920s and early 1930s the Baya organized widespread resistance against European colonists, which was brutally repressed by the French authorities. In 1960 the French withdrew and the region was granted independence, becoming the Central African Republic. The Baya today live mainly in the southwest of that country.

SOCIETY AND DAILY LIFE

The Baya are an agricultural people who cultivate cassava as their staple crop. Yams, peanuts, squashes, corn, bananas, and beans are also grown. The main domestic animals are goats and chickens. Cattle were introduced in the colonial period and are

A Baya hunter in Cameroon. Hunting and fishing are still practiced, although they now only contribute in a minor way to the diet of the Baya.

now widely kept. Many Baya now also grow cash crops for export, such as tobacco, cotton, and coffee. Others have been driven by poverty to seek work in the diamond mines of the Central African Republic.

The Baya are the CAR's largest ethnic group, making up one-third of its population. Historically they were never unified under a centralized kingdom. Before colonialism the Baya were a largely equal society, with few differences in wealth between individuals and families. The Baya

THE MYTH OF TÓ

Tó (or Wanto) is one of the most important and common figures in Baya mythology. His most important role is that of the "civilizing hero," who first introduces agriculture to humans, showing them which plants may be eaten and how grain is sown and harvested. In the legends, Tó steals the secrets of fire and water, and also domestic animals, from his father, the creator god Gbaso, and gives them to people to use. He also teaches people how to build dwellings and the art of dancing. Tó plays a major role in traditional Baya culture, and is a symbolic figure in rituals as well as in oral literature. The initiation ceremonies of young Baya men often include the Youla Tó ("Dance of Tó").

have sometimes come together temporarily under a single leader in times of crisis. Baya society is divided into clans, although each family is responsible for growing its own food. Positions of power and property are passed down the male line of inheritance.

CULTURE AND RELIGION

Baya religion includes a belief in a range of supernatural beings, such as ancestral spirits who must be appeased by sacrificial offerings to ensure success in everyday activities, such as marriage, hunting, and planting fields. There are also several powerful lesser gods, associated with nature and the elements: Kpak, for example, is the lord of all animals, while Kolo appears to humans in the form of storms. The Baya also believe in evil spirits, such as the Doua that possess people by living in their stomachs. The supreme creator-god is called Gbaso, an all-powerful sky being who rules over the other gods and who made humans. Unusually in Africa, Gbaso is not remote from human affairs and sacrifices are made to him. Colonialism brought Christianity to the Baya and many of their preexisting beliefs have been replaced by or mixed with Christian ideas. Belief in sorcery is still widespread, even among Christianized Baya.

SEE ALSO: Mbuti, Twa, and Mbenga; Metalwork; Sculpture.

BEMBA

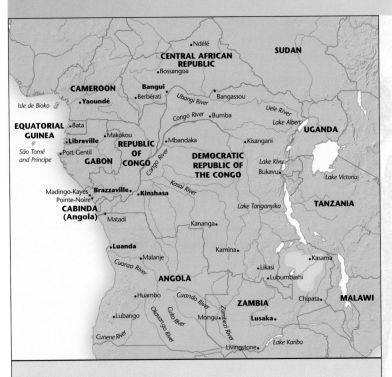

FACT FILE

Population	700,000 in northern Zambia
Religion	Christianity; preexisting Bemba practices
Language	The Bemba language Cibemba is a Bantu language of the Niger-Congo family and has many dialects. It is widely spoken in Zambia by c.3.7 million non-Bemba people as a second language.

TIMELINE

c.1650   The Bemba arrive in what is now northern Zambia.

c.1750   The Bemba begin to expand their influence over northern Zambia, forming a kingdom under a ruler known as the Chitimukulu.

1867   The British missionary, David Livingstone, passes through the Bemba area.

1889   The British South Africa Company establishes control over what is now Zambia.

1923   New Testament is translated into the Bemba language.

1924   Formation of the British colony of Northern Rhodesia.

1964   Zambia achieves independence from Britain.

1969   Recognition of the Chitimukulu's authority is withdrawn by the postindependence Zambian government.

1991   Multiparty democracy is instituted in Zambia. Frederick Chiluba, a Bemba, becomes president (until 2002).

2003   Former president Chiluba is arrested and charged with corruption.

THE UMBRELLA TERM *BEMBA* COVERS EIGHTEEN DIFFERENT BANTU GROUPS LIVING ON THE HIGH PLATEAU OF NORTHERN ZAMBIA. THESE GROUPS ARE UNITED BY THE BEMBA LANGUAGE, WHICH IS WIDELY USED IN ZAMBIA, BEING THE SECOND MOST COMMONLY SPOKEN LANGUAGE THERE, AFTER ENGLISH.

HISTORY

According to the oral history of the Bemba, they appear to have a fairly recent origin in Zambia, arriving there sometime during the mid-17th century. These stories reveal that the Bemba came from the Kola region of the present-day Democratic Republic of the Congo and are probably an offshoot of the Luba. By the end of the 18th century the Bemba had established themselves as rulers of a powerful kingdom, and were able to expand their territory throughout northern Zambia over the next hundred years.

The Bemba first encountered Europeans in the late 19th century, when the first Christian missionaries arrived in the 1880s. In 1889 Bemba lands were annexed by the British South Africa Company (BSAC) to become part of the British protectorate of Northern Rhodesia in 1924. From the 1920s on, many Bemba migrated to the Copperbelt of north-central Zambia in search of work in the mines there. Many Bemba today live in shantytowns in urban areas and suffer from high levels of unemployment, especially among young men. The HIV/AIDs epidemic is also a major problem; Zambia has the highest infection rate in Central Africa.

SOCIETY AND DAILY LIFE

The Bemba who still live in the countryside mostly grow finger millet and cassava, moving their farming plots through shifting

cultivation. Since the region that they inhabit is within the area afflicted by the tsetse fly, the risk of livestock contracting the deadly disease trypanosomasis (sleeping sickness) is high. Cattle, then, are seldom kept, though less vulnerable smaller animals such as sheep and goats are sometimes kept. Bemba villages usually consist of around 40 wattle-and-daub huts, with each family owning its own farming plot.

In the past Bemba society was based on a social system of different classes (that is, a hierarchy). At its head was the king, followed by various territorial chiefs and subchiefs. A person's status depended on which kinship group they belonged to, and whether it occupied a high or low place in the social order. The status of Bemba chiefs

Frederick Chiluba, a Bemba and president of Zambia 1991–2002. When in office, he was accused by opponents of favoring fellow Bemba in his government.

has been greatly reduced since independence. From 1969 on, the Zambian government refused to recognize the authority of the king. In addition, with many Bemba people moving to cities to find work, the villages that were the centers of chiefly power have declined in importance and size.

In the past, Bemba society was largely matrilineal—that is, individuals traced their family relationships through their mothers. Many tasks were practiced by both men and women, including fishing. Women were responsible for cooking, collecting foods, and planting crops, while men harvested, cut trees, and engaged in politics.

CULTURE AND RELIGION

Bemba religious beliefs have been heavily influenced by Christianity since the beginning of the colonial period. Many Bemba people are now Protestant, at least in name, although several preexisting religious practices are mixed with Christianity. These include showing respect to ancestral spirits called *ifkidwe*, especially those of dead chiefs, which were known as *mipashi*. The Bemba also believe in a powerful creator god called Leza, who is distant from everyday human affairs. Accordingly, religious ceremonies usually appeal to the ancestors as intermediaries rather than directly to Leza.

SEE ALSO: *Christianity; Festival and ceremony; Sculpture.*

CHISUNGU

The Bemba initiation rite that admits young girls into womanhood is known as Chisungu. The ritual lasts for about one month, with the girls being taught about giving birth, motherhood, marriage, and their future role in society. In particular the Chisungu teaches girls to respect the authority of older women. Much of the information is encoded in secret songs that pass on moral values and beliefs. The initiation is led by the *nacimba*, or mistress of ceremonies, who also acts as the midwife to the initiates when they give birth to their first child and often continues to advise them when they are married.

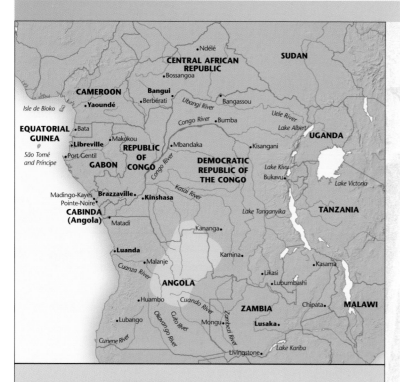

FACT FILE

Population	c.1 million Chokwe, with the largest population—0.5 million—in Angola
Religion	Chokwe religion
Language	The Chokwe language, WuChokwe, is a member of the Western Bantu branch of the Niger-Congo language family.

TIMELINE

c.1600	Split between the Lunda and Chokwe; the Chokwe settle the Kuango and Kasai rivers.
1836	Portugal officially outlaws the slave trade, although many slaves continue to be smuggled from the region.
1884–85	The Congo Free State is established by the Belgians in the northern Chokwe region. The Chokwe rebel against Lunda authority and seize control of the Lunda kingdom.
1885–1900	The Portuguese consolidate their control over the area of the Angolan interior occupied by the Chokwe.
1890s	The Lunda retake their kingdom from the Chokwe.
1920	The Chokwe expand east into what is now Zambia.
1975	Angola achieves independence, but long-running civil war erupts between MPLA regime and UNITA rebels.
1998	Fighting between UNITA and the MPLA resumes after failure of four years of ceasefire.
2002	UNITA leader Jonas Savimbi is killed, and an uneasy peace is concluded in Angola.

THE CHOKWE PEOPLE LIVE MAINLY IN NORTHEASTERN ANGOLA, AROUND THE UPPER REACHES OF THE KUANGO AND KASAI RIVERS. HOWEVER, SMALLER CHOKWE POPULATIONS INHABIT THE NEIGHBORING COUNTRIES OF THE DEMOCRATIC REPUBLIC OF THE CONGO AND ZAMBIA.

HISTORY

The Chokwe are related to the Lunda peoples, who live farther to the east. These two groups have a long history of tension and conflict. The Chokwe are believed to have developed from a group led by one of the sons of the Lunda king, which broke away from the main Lunda population in the early 17th century. Yet even after this split, the Lunda still seem to have exercised some control over the Chokwe, exacting tribute from them up until 1885, when the Chokwe gained control of the Lunda court. This victory was shortlived, however, and the Lunda managed to reassert their dominance in the 1890s.

The Chokwe were important trading partners of the Portuguese in the 19th century. At first they supplied slaves, ivory, and rubber to the Ovimbundu peoples, who acted as middlemen passing the goods on to the European colonists on the coast. When the Congo Free State was established by the Belgian King Leopold II in 1885, the slave trade declined. However, the Chokwe were now able to trade directly in ivory and rubber with the Portuguese, without using the Ovimbundu as intermediaries. Since independence in 1975, there has been tension between the Chokwe and the Angolan government, since the Chokwe believe that their lands have been exploited without any benefits for their people.

SOCIETY AND DAILY LIFE

The Chokwe have always been a mainly agricultural and rural people who use hoes to grow a variety of crops, including cassava, millet, groundnuts, yams, corn, and beans. The Chokwe living in the far south also keep small numbers of cattle, although this is not true of the Chokwe people as a whole. Hunting helps supplement the diet of the more northerly groups. Among them, hunting is a prestigious activity carried out by men, although women may help hunt smaller game animals. As a result, northern Chokwe populations tend to be less dense, with people living in smaller and more scattered villages than their southern counterparts. Women are chiefly responsible for domestic chores such as cooking, and also carry out most farming duties.

Like the Lunda people from whom they originated, the Chokwe are a hierarchical society—in other words, they have several social classes. Regional chiefs wield political authority, and attract followers to their courts through their leadership skills and political success. Wealth and power are inherited matrilineally (through the female line), so male children receive land and titles from their mother's brother, rather than from their own fathers. Also, children live with their uncle's family after they reach the age of six, rather than continuing to live at home with their parents. The Chokwe

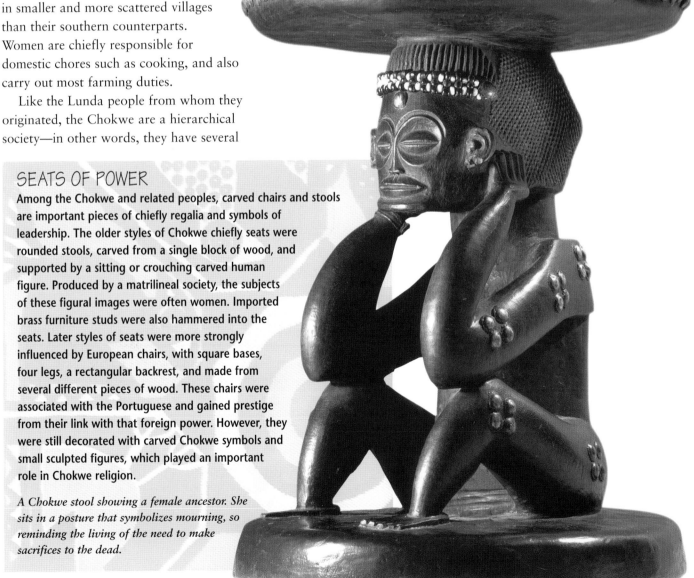

SEATS OF POWER

Among the Chokwe and related peoples, carved chairs and stools are important pieces of chiefly regalia and symbols of leadership. The older styles of Chokwe chiefly seats were rounded stools, carved from a single block of wood, and supported by a sitting or crouching carved human figure. Produced by a matrilineal society, the subjects of these figural images were often women. Imported brass furniture studs were also hammered into the seats. Later styles of seats were more strongly influenced by European chairs, with square bases, four legs, a rectangular backrest, and made from several different pieces of wood. These chairs were associated with the Portuguese and gained prestige from their link with that foreign power. However, they were still decorated with carved Chokwe symbols and small sculpted figures, which played an important role in Chokwe religion.

A Chokwe stool showing a female ancestor. She sits in a posture that symbolizes mourning, so reminding the living of the need to make sacrifices to the dead.

practice polygyny (the custom of a man having more than one wife), although it is usually restricted to the wealthier sections of rural society.

CULTURE AND RELIGION

Chokwe religion shares many of the common characteristics of other Central African societies, being based on a belief in ancestor spirits and nature spirits, which the Chokwe call *mahamba*. The Chokwe also recognize an all-powerful creator god, Kalunga, who remains distant from the everyday affairs of ordinary people. The ancestors, who are often represented by carved wooden sculptures, are shown respect with offerings to ensure that the living continue to enjoy good fortune. Each Chokwe village usually has a sacred area where the ancestors are revered, usually located near the home of the local chief. Belief in witchcraft and the negative

MUKANDA INITIATION RITES

The Chokwe male initiation ceremony is known as Mukanda. Boys between the ages of 8 and 12 take part in this rite, which is held in a secluded area away from the main village and from women. The whole process can take many years to complete.

The boys are circumcized before being taken to a special lodge where older men teach them essential lessons about the history of their people and their religious beliefs and arts. Yet unlike many other Central African initiation practices, the Chokwe Mukanda does not involve teaching practical skills like hunting. Masks are an important part of the Mukanda; they represent supernatural guides who help the initiates become men. The Mukanda masks are stored in a special building near the chief's house, and the initiation ceremony helps reinforce chiefly power.

Chokwe dancers, including a stilt-walker, perform a masquerade

(Left) A Chokwe dance mask of a type known as Mwana Pwo. *It depicts an idealized, beautiful young girl with facial scarring (scarification).*

influence of evil sorcerers is also widespread. Chiefs are often expected to have magical powers enabling them to protect their people from harmful magic.

Many Chokwe villages also have diviners known as *nganga* (who are sometimes also the village chiefs). The nganga specialize in discovering whether misfortunes have natural or supernatural causes. The diviner makes use of oracles; one such ritual involves shaking a basket full of carved ritual objects and "reading" the position they end up in as a good or bad omen for the community. These ritual objects, sometimes numbering more than sixty, may include items such as bone, ivory, wood, animal horn, nails, teeth, and small human figures. The significance of many of these objects is a closely guarded secret known only to the diviners themselves, and when the diviner dies his basket is usually destroyed. The diviners also employ rubbing-board oracles. To use this, the diviner rubs an item on a board and asks questions about the cause of a particular misfortune; the item being rubbed moves less freely when the true source is mentioned.

See also: Dance and song; Festival and ceremony; Lunda; Masks and masquerade; Ovimbundu; Sculpture.

CHRISTIANITY

TIMELINE

1483 Portuguese navigator Diogo Cão explores the mouth of the Congo River and makes contact with the kingdom of Kongo.

1491 King Nzinga of the Kongo converts to Christianity, being baptized under the name João I. The nobility follow his example, but few common people adopt the new religion.

1506–45 Christianity spreads in the kingdom of Kongo during the reign of Afonso I, who establishes regular contact with the Vatican and Portuguese bishops.

1520 Mbundu people of the Ndongo kingdom (in modern Angola) resist Portuguese attempts to convert them to Christianity.

1624–63 Reign of Dona Ana Nzinga, queen of Ndongo. Converting to Christianity to stop Portuguese slave raiding in her realm, she later splits from Portugal and fights a long guerrilla war against the colonists.

1807 Slavery is outlawed throughout the British Empire.

1839 Pope Gregory XVI issues a Papal Bull (public statement of doctrine) condemning the slave trade.

1840 The London Missionary Society sends the Scottish doctor and missionary David Livingstone to Africa to spread Christianity.

1853–54 Livingstone explores Central Africa, traveling up the Zambezi River and west to Luanda in Angola.

1883 The Paris Evangelical Mission is established among the Lozi of Barotseland (western Zambia).

1885 The White Fathers, a Catholic mission to win converts in non-Christian areas of Africa, is established in the southeastern Congo. They destroy or confiscate many pieces of indigenous religious art in the region.

1890 First Christian missions set up in Kuba territory, in the south-central Democratic Republic of the Congo.

1921 Simon Kimbangu founds the Church of Jesus on Earth through the Prophet Simon Kimbangu (*Église de Jesus sur la terre par le prophète Simon Kimbangu*) in what is now the Democratic Republic of the Congo (DRC).

1969 The Kimbanguist Church is accepted as a member of the World Council of Churches.

1990s–2000s Charismatic religious movements flourish in the war-torn DRC, including Spiritual Combat, led by Elisabeth Olangi, and the Victory Church of Fernando Kutino. Kutino's church is banned in 2002 for criticizing President Joseph's Kabila's regime.

THE CONVERSION OF THE RULERS OF THE KINGDOM OF KONGO IN THE LATE 15TH CENTURY DID NOT LEAD TO AN ENDURING OR WIDESPREAD ADOPTION OF CHRISTIANITY IN CENTRAL AFRICA. IT WAS ALMOST FOUR CENTURIES LATER BEFORE CHRISTIAN MISSIONARIES MADE A LASTING IMPRESSION ON THE REGION. TODAY, CHRISTIANITY HAS TAKEN FIRM ROOT THERE, BUT IS OFTEN MIXED WITH AFRICAN RELIGIOUS PRACTICES AND BELIEFS.

In 1483 the Portuguese explorer Diogo Cão and his small fleet of ships initiated the first formal contact between Europeans and the Central African kingdom of Kongo. Impressed by the wealth of the Portuguese and the lavish trade goods they had to offer, the ruler of Kongo soon converted to Christianity and took the name João I (d.1506). Religious objects and buildings that had been part of Kongo culture for centuries were destroyed and replaced with churches. Especially during the reign of his son Afonso I (r.1506–45), Christianity was widely adopted as the state religion of the kingdom, which became a formal Roman Catholic bishopric in 1596. However, as Portuguese influence declined, so did the importance of Christianity, and by the end of the 17th century local religious practices had once again become dominant. Yet the impact of Christianity was never entirely lost.

The island of São Tomé in the Gulf of Guinea was a key base for Christian missionary activity from the 17th century on. Roman Catholic Jesuits became active along the coast of mainland Central Africa and began translating the Bible into the region's many languages (Kikongo and

As shown in this romanticized print from the late 19th century, Christian missionaries fought against the slave trade. Yet they were also in Africa to serve the interests of colonialism and commerce.

working in Congo and Malawi respectively. Despite these early efforts to spread Christianity, the vast majority of Central Africa's population kept their preexisting religious beliefs until the colonial era.

In the late 19th and early 20th centuries mission activity increased hugely. Christian missionaries, of whom the Scot David Livingstone (1813–73) is the most famous, were often firm supporters of colonialism as well as fierce opponents of slavery. Since independence Central Africa has become one of the leading Christian regions of the world, producing many clergy who now minister both inside Africa and abroad—a reversal of the situation in the colonial era.

CHARISMATIC CHRISTIANITY

Although Roman Catholicism and Protestantism have been, and remain, the main forms of Christianity in Central Africa, the region has also given rise to its own Christian sects. Some of these have gained a wide following in a relatively short time. Such sects are usually referred to as charismatic, because they are based on the personal charisma and persuasive power of leaders who claim divine inspiration for their mission. Examples of charismatic groups

Kimbundu were the first). At the same time, Capuchin monks focused their efforts in the interior. With the transatlantic slave trade growing, many Africans were forcibly baptized as Christians in the major slave ports, such as Luanda in modern Angola, before being transported to the New World.

Protestant interest in the region began in the later 18th and 19th centuries, with groups such as the Baptist Mission Society and the Church of Scotland Mission

MBAFO ROCK SHELTER

The Mbafo rock shelter in the Democratic Republic of the Congo is one of Central Africa's more controversial archaeological sites. Its unique wall paintings are thought to date to around the 17th century, due to pottery remains that have been discovered nearby. The designs, which are mostly geometric patterns and stick figures, are clearly part of Central African artistic traditions, but some elements have been interpreted as representing Christian images. One portion resembles a cross, although this is hardly an uncommon image in many cultures and need not reflect Christian influences. Similarly there is another part that has been seen as depicting Christ being crucified. Perhaps the most convincing image is one that strongly resembles a Catholic priest in ceremonial dress, although it will probably be left for future discoveries to determine the extent to which Central African peoples had absorbed Christian ideologies at such an early date.

include the Matsouanists and Mpadists in the Republic of Congo and the Kimbanguists in the Democratic Republic of the Congo. The Kimbanguist Church was founded by the Kongo prophet Simon Kimbangu in 1921 and was at first banned by the Belgian colonial authorities before being legally recognized in 1959. Today it claims to have some four million members, making it the largest independent church in Africa. It was admitted into the World Council of Churches in 1969. Faith healing plays a major role among such groups and is an important way of recruiting followers. Another way of winning converts is to combat ancient religious practices, such as magic and witchcraft. Charismatic sects often arose as an act of resistance against colonialism, with Africans asserting their independence from European missionaries and European forms of Christianity.

A MIXTURE OF BELIEFS

The process through which Christianity has been adopted by African peoples has often been characterized by a merging of beliefs and practices from the "new" and the "old" religion to create new forms of faith. When people are introduced to the religion of a radically different culture—as happened when European Christianity was spread among Central Africans—they tend to adapt it to suit their own worldview and society. Although the kingdom of Kongo officially adopted Christianity in the 15th and 16th

Many of the outward signs of African Christianity echo European forms of the faith, as here at Lingala, DRC, where a choir poses in front of the cathedral. Yet African Christianity is often a vibrant blend of mainstream beliefs and preexisting practices.

centuries, the Christian faith did not supplant earlier beliefs but was instead blended with them, allowing the old religion to be expressed in new ways. Although a weekly mass was held in the kingdom of Kongo in accordance with Catholic custom, the ceremony was seen as a way for the king to receive the blessings of his ancestors. Similarly, baptism was seen more as a form of ritual magic that protected individuals from the threat of witchcraft and less as a cleansing of original sin and initiation into the Christian faith. Kongo understandings of Christianity later played a key role in the spread of Christianity among Africans transported to the Americas as slaves.

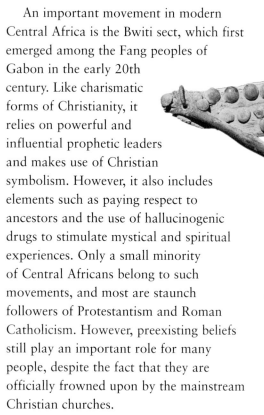

An important movement in modern Central Africa is the Bwiti sect, which first emerged among the Fang peoples of Gabon in the early 20th century. Like charismatic forms of Christianity, it relies on powerful and influential prophetic leaders and makes use of Christian symbolism. However, it also includes elements such as paying respect to ancestors and the use of hallucinogenic drugs to stimulate mystical and spiritual experiences. Only a small minority of Central Africans belong to such movements, and most are staunch followers of Protestantism and Roman Catholicism. However, preexisting beliefs still play an important role for many people, despite the fact that they are officially frowned upon by the mainstream Christian churches.

SEE ALSO: Architecture; Fang; Festival and ceremony; Kongo; Marriage and the family.

This Christ figure on this crucifix from the mid-19th century, made in wood and bronze by a local Kongo craftsman, has distinctly African features.

KONGO CRUCIFIXES

As a result of its early contact with Portuguese traders and missionaries in the 15th century, the kingdom of Kongo developed a tradition of Christian sculpture. This mainly took the form of crucifixes and figures of saints or the Virgin Mary, which are today highly prized by Western galleries and collectors. Some of the crucifixes were made of wood, with brass sections attached, while others were pure cast brass. The Christ figures produced by the Kongo often had strongly African features, in contrast to the crosses produced by European missionaries. Although influenced heavily by Christian symbolism from Catholic Europe, it is interesting to note that the cross was an important pre-Christian symbol in the kingdom of Kongo even before the arrival of Europeans in 1483. The cross symbolized a crossroads, which was itself a metaphor for the bridge between the worlds of the living and the deceased ancestors. This fact helps explain Kongo fascination with the image and their ready acceptance of the crucifix into their own visual art traditions.

ARTISTS IN CENTRAL AFRICA

Artist	Date	Country	Medium
Pilipili Mulongoye	b.1914	DRC	Paint on canvas
Lemvo Jean Abou Bakar Depara	b.1928	DRC	Paint on canvas
Leandro Mbomio Nsue	b.1938	Equatorial Guinea	Sculpture; using cast bronze
Tshibumba Kanda Matulu	1947–82	DRC	Paint on canvas
Bodys Isek Kingelez	b.1948	DRC	Sculpture; using paper, plastic, and cardboard
Monsengwo Kejwamfi ("Peintre Moke")	1950–2001	DRC	Paint on canvas
Trigo Piula	b.1950	Republic of Congo	Paint on canvas
Camille-Pierre Pambu Bodo	b.1953	DRC	Paint on canvas
Chéri Samba	b.1956	DRC	Paint on canvas
Samuel Fosso	b.1962	Central African Republic	Photography
Rigobert Nimi	b.1965	DRC	Sculpture; machined metal and electronics
Pascale Marthine Tayou	b.1967	Cameroon	Chalk and ink sketches; Video art
Barthélémy Toguo	b.1967	Cameroon	Paint on canvas, sculpture, photography

C ENTRAL AFRICA IS HOME TO A NUMBER OF CONTEMPORARY ARTISTS WITH A REPUTATION FOR CAPTURING THE VIBRANT ATMOSPHERE OF URBAN LIFE. THESE POPULAR, SELF-TAUGHT PAINTERS OFTEN COMMENT ON SOCIAL AND POLITICAL ISSUES IN THEIR ART.

URBAN ART

From the late 20th century, several Central African cities, especially Kinshasa and Lubumbashi in the Democratic Republic of the Congo (DRC), have given rise to a type of modern painting known as Urban Art. Paintings in this style typically show the realities of life in African cities, which have grown massively in size and population since independence. Urban Art deals with the daily existence of normal working people, and criticizes the effects of corruption and immorality on their lives. Artists generally paint for a local audience and are renowned for telling the viewer a clear story in their works. To this end, the painters often include text and speech captions on their paintings. Urban artists are hard-working entrepreneurs who produce hundreds of images in order to satisfy the demand for their topical pictures.

The painter Monsengwo Kejwamfi (better known as "Peintre Moke") who lived in Kinshasa, was a leading figure of this movement. His painting *Mitterrand and Mobutu* (1989), for example, shows the state visit of the former French president to Kinshasa. The artist Tshibumba Kanda Matulu from Lubumbashi was well known for his historical paintings, including a set completed in the mid-1970s that depicted the history of the Congo from ancient up to modern times, and another series, *Colonie Belge* (1973), which graphically unmasked

The Congolese artist Monsengwo Kejwamfi, who called himself "Peintre Moke," was famous for recording the buzzing city life of the capital of DRC, Kinshasa. His works were often humorous in tone, such as this self-portrait Moke Doesn't Have any Money *(1991), which shows him in threadbare clothes, being pursued by wives for support.*

the brutalities of the Belgian colonists who ruled the Congo from 1885 to 1960.

The work of Moke and other urban artists has many similarities with Central African oral literature. Urban artists tend to produce a large number of very similar pieces of art on a theme for which they have become famous. Customers often specifically request a painting that is a slight variation on another that the artist made in the past. This is very much in the storytelling tradition, where familiar themes are endlessly reworked and adapted. In contrast, Western art and literature put a premium on single pieces of work that are meant to be unique. Their creators move through many different periods of experimentation, and in doing so change their subject matter

and style. Interestingly, as their international profile has risen, some Urban Artists have turned away from narrative series of paintings in favor of "one-off" pieces.

OTHER CONTEMPORARY ARTISTS

Central Africa is also home to a large number of artists who do not belong to the Urban Art movement. Many of these painters developed their talents in Europe, where they were schooled in the Western art tradition.

One of the most well-known of Central Africa's contemporary artists is the Congolese painter Trigo Piula. Piula's work is characterized by its critical stance toward the influence of the West in Africa, and specifically the marketing of Western

Art on the move: this railroad boxcar in the Democratic Republic of the Congo has been painted with a lively mural of a contemporary scene. Moving billboards such as this are used to put across important social and health messages, such as the need to combat the spread of HIV/AIDS.

THE BIENNIAL OF CONTEMPORARY BANTU ART

Organized by the International Center for Bantu Civilizations, the first Biennial of Contemporary Bantu Art was held in Libreville, the capital of Gabon, in 1985. This exhibition has since become one of Central Africa's most important art and cultural events and has been held in several other major African cities, including Kinshasa, Brazzaville, and Bata (Equatorial Guinea). The aim of the biennial is to promote the work of modern artists from East, Central, and Southern Africa. All types of art are included and hundreds of different pieces are displayed such as paintings, sculptures, ceramics, metalwork, and engravings. Prizes ranging from U.S.$5,000 to 10,000 are awarded to the best pieces, which are assessed by an international jury of art experts and presented by the head of state of the host country. Among the Biennial's main goals are the promotion of the culture of Bantu-speaking Africa to make art more accessible to the public and to increase contacts between contemporary Bantu-speaking artists. After each Biennial, a traveling exhibition is held, which gives people in several major African cities a chance to view the artworks.

consumer goods to Africans. He also draws on older Central African art forms, such as sculpture, as a source of inspiration for his paintings. *Materna* (1984), one of Piula's best-known works, shows a seated mother and child, a common theme in the wooden sculptural traditions of the Kongo people. However in this picture, the child is black, while the mother has a white face and blonde hair. She looks straight ahead, seemingly unconcerned about the child, which appears to be dead, and is surrounded

Chéri Samba's 1994 painting Kinshasa, Ville d'ambiance (Kinshasa, a City With Atmosphere) *is typical of this popular artist's work, showing the nightlife of the Congolese capital.*

KINSHASA VIL

by empty cans of evaporated milk, an import commodity that for a long time was sold in sub-Saharan Africa by Western companies as a substitute for breast milk.

The work of the Equatorial Guinean sculptor Leandro Nbomio Nsue recalls the woodcarving traditions of the region, but also shows wider, more cosmopolitan influences. Nsue uses several media other than wood in his sculptures, for example different metals.

SEE ALSO: *Festival and ceremony; Masks and masquerade; Oral literature; Sculpture; Textiles.*

CHÉRI SAMBA

Chéri Samba, the nickname of Samba wa Mbimba N'zinga Nuni Masi Ndo Mbasi, is one of Central Africa's most prominent contemporary art figures. He was one of the founders of the Urban Art movement centered on Kinshasa. Samba gave up school in the early 1970s and became an apprentice sign painter on the streets of Kinshasa. He first began to produce his unconventional paintings in 1975. Samba's paintings are heavily influenced by comic-book art, and he often uses speech bubbles on his images. He also writes on his works, usually in either French or Lingala, in order to focus the viewer's attention clearly on the subject of the picture. Samba's international reputation was established in the 1980s, when he started to show his works in Europe and America, particularly at the "Magiciens de la terre" exhibition held in Paris in 1989. Although Samba comes from the Urban Art tradition, and likes to describe himself as an *artiste populaire* (popular artist), he has more recently begun to experiment with a wider range of styles and subjects, and to produce works primarily for the international art market. This approach is in marked contrast with his early works, which were variations on a limited repertoire of themes.

DANCE AND SONG

MAJOR CENTRAL AFRICAN SINGERS

Artist	Dates	Gender	Group	Active Period
Le Grand Kalle (Joseph Kabasele)	b.1930	Male	African Jazz	1950s–1980s
Franco (Luambo Makiadi)	b.1938	Male	OK Jazz	1950s–1980s
Tabu Ley (Tabu Pascal)	b.1940	Male	African Fiesta	1960s on
Papa Noël (Antoine Nedule Monswet)	b.1940	Male	Ok Jazz, Orchestre African Jazz	1950s on
Sam Mangwana	b.1945	Male	OK Jazz	1960s on
Pepe Kalle (Kabasele Ya Mpanya)	b.1951	Male	African Jazz	1960s–1990s
Nyoka Longo	b.1953	Male	Zaiko Langa Langa	1960s on
Papa Wemba (Shungu Jules Wembadio)	b.1953	Male	Zaiko Langa Langa	1970s on
Tshala Muana	b.1958	Female	Tsheke Tsheke	1970s on
Koffi Olomide	b.1958	Male	Quartier Latin	1980s on
Mbilia Bel	b.1959	Female	Afrisa International	1970s on

CENTRAL AFRICA HAS MANY DANCE AND SONG TRADITIONS, WHICH VARY WIDELY FROM PEOPLE TO PEOPLE. SINGING AND DANCING FORM AN INTEGRAL PART OF MANY DIFFERENT CEREMONIES AND SOCIAL OCCASIONS, INCLUDING INITIATIONS, WEDDINGS, MASQUERADES, FUNERALS, AND STORYTELLING. THEY EVEN ACCOMPANY MORE DAY-TO-DAY ACTIVITIES SUCH AS GRINDING CEREALS OR PLANTING CROPS.

Central African dance traditions are extremely diverse, ranging from the martial *mganda* dance of the Tonga of Zambia to the more gentle dances performed by the peoples of the rainforest, such as the flute dances of the Baaka of Cameroon and the Central African Republic. The *mganda* has interesting origins, developing among men who had served in the British Army during World War II (1939–45) and become skilled in military drill; the dance is performed with parade-ground movements and accompanied by strong and powerful drumbeats.

Many of the older indigenous dances and songs of Central Africa are now mainly confined to the more

Male and female dancers in the Democratic Republic of the Congo. The DRC covers a huge area of Central Africa and is home to a wide variety of peoples. Many use dance and song for festivals and ceremonies such as initiation rites, investing new chiefs or kings, and funerals.

The Mbuti rainforest people of the Democratic Republic of the Congo and Central African Republic perform the "Dance of the Bambuti," a shuffling dance to a steady drumbeat. The dancers wear leaves tied around their waists.

rural areas. Even so, the song and dance styles that catch on in cosmopolitan cities such as Brazzaville and Kinshasa were, and still are, strongly influenced by the rhythms and movements of earlier traditions.

The strict division between instrumental music and song is a Western notion. Most of the peoples of Central Africa do not regard song and dance as distinct forms of musical or artistic expression. Indeed, most cultures use the same word to describe "song," "music," and "dance."

RAINFOREST MUSIC AND THE WEST

Western musical scholars and musicians have long been interested in the polyphonic singing of the rainforest peoples of Central Africa. The first person to record this unique sound was a scholar named Hugh Tracey, who traveled into the Ituri forest in 1952 to put the music of the Mbuti people on tape for the International Library of African Music project. More recently, two French musicians, Eric Mouquet and Michel Sanchez, sampled rainforest songs from the region for their bestselling fusion album *Deep Forest* (1992). This work was widely criticized for portraying the rainforest peoples in a patronizing way as a timeless and unchanging tribal society. Moreover some of their supposedly rainforest music turned out to come from the Pacific Solomon Islands! In 1998, the British guitarist Martin Cradick, who had stayed with the Baka people of Cameroon and studied their music, formed the group "Baka Beyond" with Baka singers and players. Proceeds from their recordings have been used to benefit the Baka community, helping them buy medicines and secure land rights from neighboring peoples.

GROUP SINGING TRADITIONS

Among the peoples of Central Africa in precolonial times, singing was almost exclusively undertaken as a group activity. The idea of an individual performance was largely unknown. The choral singing of Central Africa's peoples has become justly famous for its sophistication and complexity. Although choral singing is found throughout the world, Central Africa is recognized as one of the regions where this type of performance art has reached its highest levels of development and elaboration.

Group singing is often categorized as either monophonic (where all voices sing exactly the same sound, not practiced in Central Africa), homophonic, or polyphonic. Homophonic singing is widespread in Central Africa. In this form of singing, several voices sing the same melody or tune. Although the individual voices may be singing parts that are at different levels (and can be as much as an octave apart) each part is rhythmically in step with each of the others. Homophony is found in the musical traditions of the Zande of the northeastern Democratic Republic of the Congo, along with those of many of the peoples of Angola, Malawi, and Zambia.

It is, however, polyphonic singing for which Central Africa is most celebrated. This type of music has strong associations with rainforest groups such as the Mbuti and Baka. Polyphony is multi-part singing, in which the different parts are said to be in counterpoint to each other. This means that each part consists of an independent melody with a different rhythm, and the parts combined to form a coherent, and extremely complex, musical piece. The art of polyphony is very difficult to master, and only emerged in Europe around the 13th century. The polyphonic yodeling of the rainforest groups is renowned for its haunting chords. It is often performed before sunrise, when it is believed to enchant the animals of the forest and make them fall prey more easily to bands of hunters. The rainforest peoples' singing plays an important part in their relationship with their environment. Singing is the way in which these people, who see themselves as the children of the forest, communicate with the forest and its spirits and make their needs and wishes known.

POPULAR SONG AND DANCE

Congolese rumba is the most widespread form of popular dance music in Central Africa. This style emerged in Kinshasa and Brazzaville in the second half of the 20th century, and has since gained a widespread following across Africa and beyond. It was among the young in the dance halls of the 1960s that rumba first found its mass market, which has grown rapidly over the following decades. Also known as soukous, the Congolese rumba is distinctive for its highly rhythmic dances, which combine elements of both African and Cuban styles,

THE INDEPENDENCE CHA CHA CHA

The Congolese rumba developed during a politically tense period in Central African history, as the colonial period was drawing to a close and the first self-governing African states were emerging. The "Independence Cha-Cha-Cha," released in 1960, was a product of this heady atmosphere of rapid change. This song was written by the band African Jazz, led by Joseph Kabele, and performed for the first time at a conference in Brussels where the final negotiations on the handover of power from the Belgian colonial authorities to the newly formed government of Congo (Kinshasa) were taking place. It perfectly captured the public mood of the time, expressing a feeling of hope and optimism for the future that was shared by many Africans. On Independence Day itself, Patrice Lumumba, the first prime minister of Congo (Kinshasa) delivered an impassioned speech fiercely attacking the legacy of Belgian colonialism, and followed it by defiantly playing a recording of the "Independence Cha-Cha-Cha," in the presence of the unamused king of Belgium.

characterized by subtle movements of the hips and arms. Congolese rumba is sung passionately in either French or Lingala, an important Bantu "lingua franca" (a common language used by many) in the region. It has produced some internationally famous bands and superstar singers, including groups like OK Jazz, African Jazz, and Les Bantous de la Capitale. There are also a number of famous female singers in this style, such as Mbilia Bel, who led the way for a generation of African women superstars in the 1980s. Despite the influence of Latin American and Western dance music, Congolese rumba has always maintained a strongly African flavor, and its origins in indigenous African song and dance are evident. Soukous singers often record many different versions of the same song rather than repeating the original version. This "variation on a theme" approach is common to other creative traditions in Central Africa, such as storytelling and popular painting.

SEE ALSO: Contemporary art; Festival and ceremony; Masks and masquerade; Mbuti, Twa, and Mbenga; Music and musical instruments; Oral literature.

The Congolese singer Kanda Bongo Man (b.1955), seen here at a "Live 8" concert in 2005, is a highly popular entertainer who tours worldwide. He sings in Lingala, and his form of soukous has given rise to a lively dance form called kwassa kwassa.

MAJOR WORKS AND THEIR AUTHORS

Title	Date	Author	Country
Zambia Shall Be Free	1962	Kenneth Kaunda	Zambia
Before Dawn	1970	Andreya Masiye	Zambia
Tongue of the Dumb	1971	Dominic Mulaisho	Zambia
Victims of Fate	1972	Gideon Phiri	Zambia
Africa is Made of Clay	1975	Patu Simoko	Zambia
The Smoke That Thunders	1979	Dominic Mulaisho	Zambia
Bwana District Commissioner: White Colonial Master	1989	Kapasa Makasa	Zambia
Quills of Desire	1993	Binwell Sinyangwe	Zambia
A Referendum of Forest Creatures	1993	Steve Chimombo	Malawi
Murder in the Forest	1998	Grieve Sibale	Zambia
A Cowrie of Hope	2000	Binwell Sinyangwe	Zambia
The Wrath of Napolo	2000	Steve Chimombo	Malawi

Zambia's first president, Kenneth Kaunda (b.1924), was the author of seven works about the political life of his country. Many of the first wave of African leaders after independence were also respected writers.

ENGLISH IS THE LEAST WIDELY SPOKEN EUROPEAN LANGUAGE IN CENTRAL AFRICA, WHICH IS DOMINATED BY FRENCH AND PORTUGUESE. LITERATURE IN THIS LANGUAGE IS THEREFORE LARGELY CONFINED TO ZAMBIA.

Before the country finally achieved independence in 1964 and adopted the name Zambia, it was a part of the British Empire known as Northern Rhodesia. Today, English is still an officially recognized language in Zambia and is the language used in school education.

HISTORICAL DEVELOPMENT AND MAIN AUTHORS

The first English-language literature in Central Africa appeared during the 1960s and 1970s. As with much postcolonial literature throughout Africa, these early writings were mainly concerned to point out the negative effects of colonialism and to promote the struggle for independence. Zambia's first president, Kenneth Kaunda, who was a politician as well as a writer (a common feature in several Central African countries) wrote the autobiography *Zambia Shall be Free* in 1962. This work mixed details from Kaunda's own life with an account of the role played by the Zambian independence movement in building a nation free from European control. Many early novels were fiercely critical of the Western world and its influence in Africa. Notable among these was *Tongue of the Dumb* (1969) by the Zambian economist and writer Dominic Mulaisho (b.1933). This work showed the clash between African and Western culture, in particular European efforts to convert African peoples to Christianity and to persuade them to abandon their own religious beliefs.

Since the 1970s the output of English-language literature has increased sharply. This has gone hand in hand with an ever greater diversity of themes and approaches. Across Central Africa as a whole, many postindependence writers have voiced their bitter disappointment that the end of colonialism did not bring solutions for Africa's problems. Zambia was a one-party state under Kaunda's United National Independence Party from independence right up to the 1990s. However, its people were not subjected to the harsh dictatorial repression that affected a number of other Central African states, and so political writings criticizing the government were less common there than elsewhere. Even so, some Zambian writers, including Mulaisho, have attacked the corruption and unfairness of postcolonial society in their works.

Recent literature from the region has tackled wider themes, such as the relations between men and women. It has also become more experimental, making use of mythology and complex allegories. *The Heart of Women* (1997), a collection of writings by the Zambian Women Writers' Association, deals with the problems that can arise in male–female relationships, particularly domestic violence. The Malawian author Steve Chimombo, who writes mainly on the subject of Zambia, makes extensive use of myth, as for example in his novel *A Referendum of Forest Creatures*, which exposes the injustices of repressive government. Another popular writer is Grieve Sibale, whose *Murder in the Forest* is a gripping tale about the murder of a poor immigrant by a wealthy businessman.

SEE ALSO: African-language literature; French-language literature; Movies; Oral literature.

(Above) Quills of Desire, *about an ambitious school student, was the first novel by the Zambian writer Binwell Sinyangwe (b.1956). Steve Chimombo's novel* The Wrath of Napolo *is one of a series of writings by this author about a mythical serpent.*

STEVE CHIMOMBO

Steve Chimombo was born in Zomba, Malawi, in 1945. He studied in the United States and the United Kingdom before returning to Africa to become professor of English at the University of Malawi. He is today one of the country's best known playwrights, novelists, and poets and was awarded the Commonwealth poetry prize in 1987. Chimombo is noted for his extensive use of Zambian oral tradition and mythology, which runs right through his written works. Napolo, a magical creature who lives underground, is one of his most frequently used characters. He appears in much of Chimombo's poetry from the 1980s as well as in his recent novel *The Wrath of Napolo* (2000), which is an allegory of the advent of multiparty democracy to Zambia (an allegory is a tale that uses a fantasy situation to symbolize and criticize real-life events).

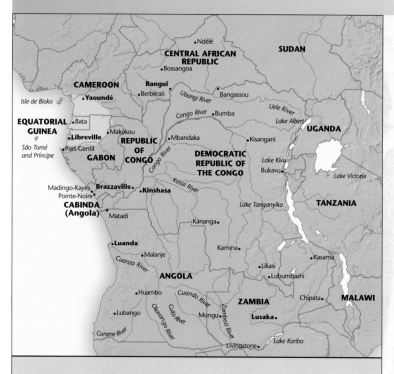

FACT FILE

Population	c.0.6 million, mainly in Equatorial Guinea, where they make up most of the population; 110,000 in Cameroon
Religion	Christianity; Bwiti
Language	The Fang language is a Bantu language of the Niger-Congo language family.

TIMELINE

c.800s   The Fang settle northern Cameroon.

1472 onward   Ndowe sell captured Fang to the Portuguese on Fernando Póo island (now Bioko) in the Gulf of Guinea.

1520s   The Portuguese set up slave-trading ports in Cameroon.

c.1800   Fang begin to migrate south of the Sanaga River, into southern Cameroon, Gabon, and Equatorial Guinea.

1844   Spanish settle mainland Equatorial Guinea (Río Muni).

1884   Germany establishes the colony of Kamerun.

1910   French Equatorial Africa is formed, including Gabon.

1926   In Cameroon, the Fang form the Elarayong Movement, an anticolonial resistance organization.

1960–61   Gabon and then Cameroon achieve independence.

1968   Spanish Guinea wins independence as Equatorial Guinea, led by Macias Nguema, a Fang of the Esangui clan.

1979   Nguema is killed in a coup led by his nephew Obiang.

2004   Planned coup by mercenaries to oust Obiang fails.

THE FANG ARE A BANTU PEOPLE WHO INHABIT NORTHWESTERN GABON, EQUATORIAL GUINEA, AND A SMALL SECTION OF SOUTHERN CAMEROON. THE AREA WHERE THEY LIVE IS LARGELY COVERED WITH EQUATORIAL RAINFOREST. THEY ARE INFLUENTIAL IN THE POLITICAL LIFE OF GABON AND EQUATORIAL GUINEA.

HISTORY

The origins of the Fang people are uncertain, but it is thought that they settled in their present location as a result of a series of migrations from the savanna grasslands of Cameroon between the 18th and early 20th centuries. From the 16th century until the colonial period many Fang were captured and sold as slaves by the Ndowe people, who acted as middlemen to Portuguese traders. To justify their actions, the Ndowe spread rumors that the Fang were uncivilized cannibals. In the later 19th century the Fang area was divided up among the various colonial powers, with the creation of the French colony of Gabon and the German colony of Kamerun. The Spanish had long maintained a trading post on the coast of this region, and from the late 19th century they also controlled the mainland enclave of Río Muni (now part of Equatorial Guinea). After World War I (1914–18) and the defeat of Germany, Kamerun was taken over by France and Britain, with most of it becoming part of French Equatorial Africa.

Under the French colonial administration of Gabon and Cameroon, the Fang occupied a number of senior positions in government and the military. However, the colonial regime in Spanish Equatorial Guinea regarded the Fang as a backward people and so allowed them little responsibility or influence. Several attempts were made to

A Fang girl pumping water from a well in Equatorial Guinea. The Fang are the dominant ethnic group in the mainland part of this small state, and have held power since independence.

organize resistance to the colonial powers in the early 20th century, such as the Elarayong Movement, founded in Cameroon. Gabon and Cameroon were not decolonized until the early 1960s, while Equatorial Guinea became independent in 1968. After independence the Fang became one of the dominant ethnic groups of the region, especially in Gabon and Equatorial Guinea, where they had great influence in postindependence governments. The Esangui clan's domination of Equatorial Guinea has been particularly brutal, and efforts to develop multiparty politics there have failed.

SOCIETY AND DAILY LIFE

The Fang are a farming people, who until the late 20th century grew and lived on yams, manioc, corn, plantains, and groundnuts, which they cultivated for their

THE NOTORIOUS NGUEMA

Born into the Esangui clan of the Fang in the Mongomo region of Equatorial Guinea in 1924, Francisco Macías Nguema became his country's first leader. He rose to prominence under the Spanish colonial regime and was appointed president with their support just before independence in 1968. Nguema soon gained a reputation for brutality. His regime conducted a widespread terror campaign. In an effort to avoid execution or torture almost one-third of Equatorial Guinea's population fled to neighboring Gabon. Nguema promoted other members of his clan to positions of power; the Esangui still form the political elite today. The excesses of his rule finally led to his overthrow in 1979 by his nephew, Teodoro Obiang Nguema Mbasogo, who has clung to power ever since despite calls for democratic change.

own consumption (subsistence farming). Men were responsible for clearing agricultural land, while their wives planted the crops. In the more isolated areas of the forest Fang men still hunt, an activity that was much more common in the past. The Fang have generally not raised large numbers of cattle due to the high risk of infection with the disease trypanosomasis (sleeping sickness) spread by the tsetse fly. However,

new breeds of cattle resistant to the disease were introduced to Gabon in the 1980s, and some Fang are now engaged in herding.

In the past, all Fang lived in villages consisting of related males and their wives and children, with each family unit cultivating their own fields. Forest was regularly cleared by the shifting cultivation method, and villages would gradually migrate to new areas over time. Today, with the introduction of cash crops such as coffee and cocoa, subsistence agriculture has largely given way to growing crops for export. Consequently, the Fang now have a money economy and live in more permanent settlements or on plantations. Slash-and-burn techniques are still used, and the ground is prepared for planting using hoes. Imported and mass-produced foodstuffs, including canned sardines, bread, and condensed milk, and household goods are widely traded at regular markets. Yet it is no longer the case that all Fang are employed in agriculture, and many of the population now live in towns. Bioko Island, off the coast of Equatorial Guinea, is the administrative center of Equatorial Guinea and many urban Fang live there, forming a wealthy elite.

A Fang harp made of wood and leather and decorated with a carved head.

KU MÉLAN INITIATION RITES

The initiation rite for young Fang men, through which they become a full member of their clan, is known as Ku Mélan. The group of initiates withdraw from their village to a separate, purpose-built camp. There, a band is assembled to provide music with xylophones and drums. The *bieri* (reliquaries holding the remains of the ancestors) also play an important part in the initiation ceremony and are kept at the camp. During the ceremony the initiates eat the bark of the *alan* plant, which gives them hallucinatory dreams in which they see the ancestors. After they wake from their dreams the young men describe their visions to the diviner, who interprets what they have seen and determines what sorts of foods or activities are taboo for each individual. A major part of the Ku Mélan rites is the teaching of a person's ancestry, so that each initiate understands who his own forebears were.

CULTURE AND RELIGION

Belief in witches and sorcery forms a major part of Fang religion. Misfortune is often seen as being the result of sorcery. Although many Fang today have embraced Christianity, it is interpreted in terms of the Fang's own culture. For example, the Christian idea of sin is translated in the Fang language as *nsem*, which also means "witchcraft." Witches (*nném*) are thought to be possessed by a vampiric spirit known as an *évus*. They are accused of committing all kinds of terrible deeds, including sacrificing members of their own family and consuming their remains. Witchcraft can be combated by seeking the help of a *ngengang*, a respected community healer and diviner.

In common with many other Central African societies, the Fang religion involves communicating with and showing respect to ancestors. Ancestral spirits are thought to help the living solve the problems they encounter in everyday life. People offer up prayers to these spirits in the hope that they will be blessed with success in marriage, hunting, or warfare. The ancestor spirits are represented by wooden figures called *bieri* that were attached to reliquaries (caskets) holding the skeletal remains of the dead ancestors, especially their skulls and long bones. Because only the human remains are regarded as sacred, many *bieri* have been sold to Western art dealers.

The Fang religion also involves the worship of a supreme creator god called Mebere. Mebere is believed to have created all things, including Nzame, the first man, and (from one of his toes) Nyingo Mebere, the first woman. The idea of ancestral spirits has been merged with Christianity to form the Bwiti cult (see CHRISTIANITY), a sect that emerged among the Fang in the early 20th century.

Until the colonial period the Fang did not belong to any centralized state or kingdom. Clans were once a major part of Fang society and people were expected to marry outside of their own clan group, but today they play a less important role. The Fang practice polygyny (the custom of a man having more than one wife). However, marriage requires a payment of bridewealth by the husband to the woman's family, and so it is only wealthier men who can afford to support more than one wife. Fang society is primarily patrilineal, meaning that inheritance occurs along the male line, from father to son.

A Fang wooden helmet mask from Gabon. This mask was used by the Ngongtang society in rituals to dispel the evil influence of witchcraft.

SEE ALSO: *Christianity; Festival and ceremony; Masks and masquerade; Mbuti, Twa, and Mbenga; Sculpture.*

MAJOR EVENTS IN CENTRAL AFRICA

Lozi of the Zambezi Valley	The Kuomboka festival takes place each year when the Zambezi River floods. The king and his subjects migrate to high ground above the floodplain, amid music and dancing. The festival is held again when the king returns to the lowlands.	February–May, according to the king's judgement
Chokwe and related peoples	Mukanda is the most common form of initiation for boys, and takes place across Central Africa. The initiates are withdrawn from the village and taught secret historical and ritual knowledge.	When boys are of the right age for initiation (8–12 years)
Lunda of Zambia	The Umutomboko (meaning "victory") celebrates the migration of the Lunda's ancestors into Zambia from the north and the many successful battles they fought along the way. It lasts for two days, and includes feasting, speeches, music, and animal sacrifices.	July
Mbenga of the Congo Basin	The Mobandi is a seasonal ritual in which participants beat themselves with branches in an attempt to attract evil and misfortune onto themselves and therefore protect the community at large from harm.	Before the the rainy season
Tonga of S Zambia	The Lwiinde Gombe festival is an occasion at which thanks and ritual offerings are given to the ancestors. The ceremony is attended by many chiefs from the surrounding area.	July
Kaonde of NW Zambia	The Kufukwila is a major royal festival, in which the Kaonde people show their respect and pay homage to their ruler. The festival involves feasting and dancing.	May

CENTRAL AFRICA HAS A HUGE NUMBER OF CEREMONIES AND FESTIVALS. SONGS, STORYTELLING, DANCE, MASQUERADING, AND MUSIC OFTEN FORM A MAJOR PART OF THESE TRADITIONAL RITUALS. OTHER, MORE MODERN FESTIVALS CELEBRATE DIFFERENT ASPECTS OF THE REGION'S SOCIAL AND CULTURAL LIFE.

RITES OF PASSAGE

The term *rites of passage* is used to describe a special class of rituals and ceremonies that focus on important changes in every individual's life. All societies around the world mark these key stages in some way. They may include the process of becoming an adult, getting married, or becoming a parent for the first time. Each of these phases involves a transition and a change in a person's status. Most cultures do not even regard death as a full-stop, but rather believe that a person becomes one of the ancestors when they die or enters an afterlife. Accordingly, the end of life is simply treated as just another rite of passage, another move from one state of being to the next. In Central Africa, African rites of passage have been joined by those imported through Western influence, notably Christian ceremonies such as baptism and confirmation, or even nonreligious ceremonies such as college graduation.

Initiation is one of the most universal rites of passage found in Central Africa. All peoples of the region see adulthood as a state that entails a wide range of different

An Ovimbundu dancer from Huila province, Angola, taking part in a ceremony during which boys are circumcised.

The Mukanda initiation ceremony is an extremely important ritual of the Chokwe. It involves a masquerade of the makishi, *ancestor spirits who return to the land of the living to offer guidance.*

rights and responsibilities. Initiations are always gender-specific, meaning that boys and girls are never initiated together. Central African cultures generally view men and women as occupying quite different roles in society, and as possessing different kinds of knowledge. Some societies, such as the Lozi and the Bemba, only have female initiation ceremonies, while others have initiations for boys only. However, it is most common for a people to have both male and female initiation traditions. Initiations vary from place to place, although it is common for the initiates to be separated from the rest of the community for several months, while they are told ancient stories and taught key skills to prepare them for their life as adults.

Masks and dances are also extremely common features of initiations. Each culture usually has a series of specific masks that are reserved solely for use in initiation ceremonies. There may also be a special class of objects associated with initiation, such as the chief's *mukupele* drum of the Chokwe, which may only be played at the initiation ceremonies for boys.

Funerary rites are of great significance in Central African cultures, and in most cases are designed to allow the living to continue to have an ongoing relationship with the deceased (the ancestors). Carved figures for holding the physical remains of the dead, known as reliquaries, are widespread, such as the *bieri* of the Fang, or the *muzidi* of the Bembe (a Kongo subgroup). They provide a focus for ceremonies and rituals in which the ancestors are contacted and given offerings. These rites illustrate how the dead continue to play an important role in society after they have departed from the world of the living. There is a major difference between the funerary rites of chiefs and kings on the one hand, which are often the occasion of great ceremony and animal sacrifices, and the much simpler ceremonies of commoners. Among the Kongo, textiles were an

THE MOBANDI CEREMONY

Although seasonal rites are most common in agricultural (crop-growing) societies, they can be important to hunter-gatherer peoples as well. The Mobandi ceremony is a ritual occasion that is celebrated by the Mbenga (or Aka) peoples who live in the equatorial rainforests of the Republic of Congo and the Central African Republic. The ceremony takes place once every year after the flowering of the *mbaso* tree, which is considered sacred by several Central African cultures, and before the onset of the rainy season. During the ceremony some of the Mbenga beat themselves with branches. They believe that this helps them absorb evil forces, known as *kose*, that might otherwise do harm to the rest of the community. The ceremony is associated with the collection of honey, which takes place after the Mobandi, and it is believed that the ritual cleansing that takes place will ensure that the spirits help bring about a plentiful honey harvest. This is the only seasonal ritual that is celebrated by the Mbenga.

important part of the often very elaborate funeral rites that took place in the early colonial period. High-status individuals were wrapped in expensive fabrics after death, including raffia and imported linens, cottons, and silks. This would create an enormous bundle that was many times larger than the body contained within it. The richness of the cloths indicated how important the person had been in life. The top of the bundle was frequently shaped to look like a small head, so as to give the body a vaguely human appearance. Before the body was buried, there would be dancing and other ceremonial activities.

OTHER CEREMONIES AND FESTIVALS

A number of other important ceremonies take place in Central Africa to mark the change of the seasons, and other aspects of the agricultural cycle. The Lozi king, for example, moves annually from his home on the Zambezi plains to his home on higher ground when the rains bring seasonal floods. The return of the king to the plains is a major ceremonial occasion and is greeted by dancing and celebrations. Royal festivals linked to the agricultural cycle are still practiced by many Central African peoples.

The Baka are a hunter-gatherer people of Cameroon and the Central African Republic. One of their key festivals is the long Jengi initiation rite. Here, drummers and dancers prepare for the Jengi.

The region also boasts many festivals of a more modern origin, including arts, music, and film events. Governments may sponsor such occasions as a way of fostering national and cultural unity in countries that are composed of many different ethnic groups. Political ceremonies such as independence days have also become important since the end of colonial rule, and often involve lavish military parades. Most Central African countries host a wide range of cultural festivities, such as musical performances and displays of dancing and drumming.

SEE ALSO: Chokwe; Dance and song; Masks and masquerade; Music and musical instruments.

THE FUNERAL OF KING LEWANIKA

A description of the funeral of King Lewanika, the Lozi sovereign who died in 1916, was recorded by two Western scholars who were visiting the area at the time. Their report provides a detailed, eyewitness account of the royal funerary rites of the Lozi in the early 20th century. The king was carried to his burial place on a barge, and placed in a huge grave that was more than 30 feet (9 m) wide, along with many of his most valued possessions. The grave was only filled in that evening, after the Europeans had left, and it is possible that human sacrifices may have taken place at that point, a practice that would have attracted strong disapproval from the colonial authorities who ruled over the Lozi at that time. After the funeral, 80 cattle were sacrificed in the Lozi capital and all the fires there were put out. Later still, and as a symbol of the handover of power to the new king, Lewanika's heir kindled a new fire that was used to relight all the other fires across the capital.

FRENCH-LANGUAGE LITERATURE

MAJOR WORKS AND THEIR AUTHORS

Title	Date	Author	Country
Le Mauvais Sang (Bad Blood)	1955	Tchicaya U Tam'si	DRC
Feu de Brousse (Brush Fire)	1957		
A Triche-Coeur (A Game of Cheat-Heart)	1960		
Epitome	1960		
Le Pauvre Christ de Bomba (The Poor Christ of Bomba)	1956	Mongo Beti	Cameroon
Main Basse sur le Cameroun (Rape of Cameroon)	1972		
Perpétue et l'Habitude de Malheur (Perpetuity and the Habit of Unhappiness)	1974		
La Ruine presque Cocasse d'une Polichinelle (The Nearly Comical Ruin of a Puppet)	1979		
Trop de Soleil tue l'Amour (Too Much Sun Kills Love)	1972		
Une Vie de Boy (Life of a Houseboy)	1956	Ferdinand Oyono	Cameroon
Le Vieux Nègre et la Médaille (The Old Man and the Medal)	1956		
Chemin d'Europe (Road to Europe)	1960		
Trois Prétendants...Un Mari (Three Suitors...One Husband)	1962	Guillaume Oyono-Mbia	Cameroon
Un Fusil dans le Main, Un Poème dans la Poche (A Rifle in the Hand, A Poem in the Pocket)	1973	Emmanuel B. Dongala	DRC
Jazz et Vin de Palme (Jazz and Palm Wine)	1982		
Johnny Chien Méchant (Johnny Mad Dog)	2002		
Elonga (Elonga)	1986	Angèle N. Rawiri	Gabon
Fureurs et Cris de Femmes (Furies and Cries of Women)	1989		
Seul le Diable le savait (Only the Devil Knew)	1990	Calixthe Beyala	Cameroon
Femme Nue, Femme Noire (Naked Woman, Black Woman)	2003		
La Plantation (The Plantation)	2005		
Les Tâches d'Encre (The Ink Stains)	2002	Bessora	Gabon

FRENCH IS ONE OF THE MOST WIDELY SPOKEN LANGUAGES IN CENTRAL AFRICA, ESPECIALLY AMONG THE EDUCATED AND CITY-DWELLING CLASSES. WRITERS FROM CAMEROON, THE REPUBLIC OF CONGO, THE DEMOCRATIC REPUBLIC OF THE CONGO, AND GABON HAVE ALL PUBLISHED MAJOR LITERARY WORKS IN FRENCH.

FRENCH-LANGUAGE LITERATURE UNDER COLONIALISM

The areas occupied by the present-day countries of the Republic of Congo, Gabon, and Cameroon were colonized by France in the late 19th and early 20th centuries. They formed part of the huge territory known as French Equatorial Africa. The one French-speaking country not under French rule was the Democratic Republic of the Congo, which was the personal colony of King Leopold II of Belgium from 1885 to 1908, and from then until independence under the control of the Belgian state. French remained the official language of all these countries even after independence in 1960.

The earliest French literary works from the region, in the early 20th century, were either faithful records of stories that had long been part of local oral traditions, or were loosely based on such stories. Yet it was not long before Central African writers came under the influence of a new and more widely based intellectual trend. This movement, which was given the name negritude, emphasized black identity and was highly critical of the colonial system and its effects on the peoples of Africa. The French style of colonial government (as compared to, say, that of the British) placed great stress on assimilation. This meant that people under French colonial rule were

A newsstand in Gabon displays a wide selection of magazines. Several fiction writers have come from this region, but French-language publishing is stronger in West Africa, where economic conditions are more favorable.

expected to give up their own culture in favor of adopting French attitudes and outlook. The colonies were supposed to become part of *France outre-mer* ("France overseas"). The work of these early writers was a protest against assimilation.

Figures such as Mongo Beti (1932–2001) and Guillaume Oyono-Mbia (b.1939), of Cameroonian descent, were prominent in

THE NEGRITUDE MOVEMENT

Negritude was a literary and intellectual movement started in Paris in the 1930s by French-speaking black students from African countries and the Caribbean. The term was derived from the Latin word *nigritudo*, which means "blackness." The negritude movement was founded to promote the idea that black culture and heritage should be created and defined by black peoples themselves. Its followers firmly rejected the identities and roles that had been imposed on them by white colonialists. Although it first emerged in France, the idea of negritude rapidly spread to North America and Africa, particularly among French-speaking writers. In Africa, the term is often applied to certain works of literature from the pre-independence era. Writings by members of the negritude movement have a strong anticolonial message and reaffirm African beliefs and values in the face of Western or other influences.

anticolonial and antiracist literature throughout the early to mid-20th century. The dominant themes during this early period include the decline in "traditional" African beliefs and culture brought about by Western missionary activity and the plight of poor people and their loss of dignity under colonial rule.

LITERATURE AFTER COLONIALISM

From the 1970s a new phase began, in which widespread disappointment arose with the corruption of postcolonial governments and their failure to represent the interests of wider society. Central African nations have suffered from frequent episodes of political instability and violent oppression by dictatorial regimes. Many Central African writers were imprisoned or exiled by the regimes of their native countries. For example, the Congolese writer Emmanuel Boundzek Dongala (b.1941) has become well-known for his attacks on the abuses of power in the postcolonial world. He is particularly well known for his short stories, including his collection entitled *Jazz et vin de palme* (1982).

Some writers of the postindependence period have reacted against any attempt to idealize precolonial Africa as a kind of paradise that was destroyed by the arrival of Europeans. This theme comes through strongly in Dongala's work. Yet despite the shift of attention toward homegrown problems, the influence of the West in Africa has not been neglected as a subject by modern writers. The Congolese novelist, poet, and playwright Tchicaya U Tam'si (1931–88) voiced his frustration with the unequal economic relations that exist between Africa

MONGO BETI

Mongo Beti was the pen name of one of Cameroon's most influential novelists and political writers, Alexandre Biyidi-Awala. His early works took a strongly anticolonial stance, and from the 1970s he also began to attack corrupt postindependence regimes. In particular he was a major opponent of Ahmadou Ahidjo's government in Cameroon which kept an iron grip on power from 1960 until 1982. As a result, his books were originally banned in his home country and he lived in exile in France before returning to Cameroon in the 1990s. In 1978 Beti founded a bimonthly journal called *Peuples Noirs/Peuples Africains* ("Black Peoples/ African Peoples"), which was devoted to exposing and attacking the neocolonial influence of the West in Africa. His postindependence writings often combined a range of different themes, such as in his novel *Perpétue et l'habitude du malheur* (1974) which tells of a bright young woman whose life is destroyed by the injustices both of neocolonialism and traditional culture and attitudes.

The writer Mongo Beti was educated in a Catholic mission school in Cameroon, and later in France. His novel Le Pauvre Christ de Bomba *showed the destructive influence of Western missionaries, despite their good intentions.*

and the former colonial powers. Unlike many earlier writers, U Tam'si did not attempt to speak on behalf of all Africans, but rather focused on the plight and suffering of the poor.

Although women writers were active in Central Africa since the 1960s, they have become much more prominent in recent decades, producing a large number of works that treats the themes of different gender roles and feminism. Calixthe Beyala (b.1960), a Cameroonian who now lives in France, is known for her writings such as *Seul le Diable le savait* (1990), which criticizes the entrenched male-dominated culture of Central Africa and the disadvantages faced by women in many African societies.

SEE ALSO: *African-language literature; English-language literature; Oral literature; Portugese-language literature.*

This painting by the Congolese artist Chéri Samba, The Confused *(1995), shows Africans bombarded by moral rules from the West in French and English.*

KONGO

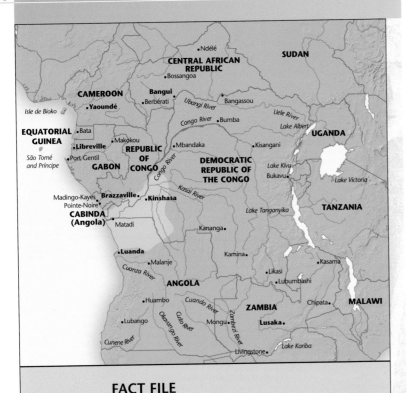

FACT FILE

Population	c.10.9 million; 9 million in DRC, 1.5 million in the Republic of the Congo, and 0.4 million in Angola
Religion	Preexisting beliefs; Christianity (Roman Catholicism)
Language	Kikongo is a Bantu language of the Niger-Congo language family. Kilela is the most widespread dialect.

TIMELINE

1300s   Rise of the Kongo kingdom in the lower Congo region.

1483   Portuguese sailor Diogo Cão visits Congo River estuary.

1491   The *mani kongo*, Afonso I, and the Kongo aristocracy, the *mwissikongo*, convert to Christianity.

1520s   Kongo kingdom begins to trade slaves with Portugal.

1568–71   Neighboring Jaga invade Kongo territory.

1596   Kongo kingdom is made a Roman Catholic bishopric.

1665   Portuguese invade and subdue the Kongo Kingdom.

1883–85   Much of the former kingdom of Kongo is incorporated into Portuguese Angola, with the rest divided between the Congo Free State (Belgium) and the French Congo.

1960–61   The two Congolese republics gain independence from France and Belgium. Bakongo lead first raids against the Portuguese authorities in Angola.

1975   Angola achieves independence from Portugal but descends into civil war.

2002   The Angolan civil war finally ends.

BY THE TIME OF FIRST EUROPEAN CONTACT IN 1483, THE KONGO KINGDOM WAS A MAJOR REGIONAL POWER. THE KONGO NOW LIVE ACROSS A VERY WIDE AREA OF CENTRAL AFRICA.

HISTORY

The Kongo people (or BaKongo) are the descendants of Bantu speakers who migrated into the region between c. 1000 B.C.E. and 500 C.E. The kingdom of Kongo emerged from the 14th century. In 1486, emissaries from the Portuguese royal court met the *mani kongo* (king). Throughout the rest of the 15th and most of the 16th century, the two kingdoms had extensive trade links with one another. Kongo also quickly embraced Christianity, with the *mani kongo* Afonso I (d.1545) adopting Roman Catholicism as the official state religion.

From the late 1500s on, however, the relationship between Portugal and the kingdom of Kongo deteriorated, as Portuguese slavers led raids into the Kongo. A full-scale invasion of the Kongo area was launched by Portugal in 1655. Despite fierce resistance, the decisive Portuguese victory at the battle of Ambuila spelt the end of Kongo self-rule. After this Christianity began to fade. In the late 19th and early 20th centuries, the Kongo region was divided between the French Congo (now the Republic of Congo), Portuguese Angola, and the Congo Free State (later the Belgian Congo and now the Democratic Republic of the Congo).

The Kongo played a leading role in the Congolese independence movements. The Kongo were also heavily involved in the liberation struggle in Angola.

SOCIETY AND DAILY LIFE

Today the Kongo are the dominant ethnic group in both the Congo republics and in Angola, with many rising to prominent

positions. They are among the most literate and urban groups in the region. Many Kongo have moved to major cities such as Kinshasa and Brazzaville to find work. Yet a large population still live in villages, growing manioc as their staple food as well as corn, peanuts, beans, cassava, peppers, and other crops. Women do most of the farm work, while men are responsible for hunting. Women trade agricultural goods at weekly markets throughout the Kongo region.

The Kongo have not been ruled by a *mani kongo* for over a century, but in rural areas local leaders and chiefs still exercise authority. Unlike many other peoples of Central Africa, the Kongo regard themselves as a unified cultural group. This is likely the result of their long history of living in a

Kongo women and children set fish-basket traps on the fast-flowing Congo River. Both men and women take part in fishing to supplement the community's diet.

centralized state. Their unity has ensured that they have major political influence in the post-independence states of Central Africa.

CULTURE AND RELIGION

Kongo beliefs focus on ancestral spirits. People make offerings to their ancestors at family shrines to try and gain favor. Roman Catholicism came early to the Kongo. By 1650 the Kongo capital, Mbanza Kongo, boasted a dozen churches and a Jesuit college. Christianity declined as Portuguese influence waned, but was reintroduced in the colonial period. The main religious movement among the Kongo combining Christian and preexisting beliefs is the Kimbanguist Church, founded by the prophet Simon Kimbangu (1889–1951), who was jailed for life by the Belgian authorities.

Many Kongo were among the millions of Africans shipped as slaves to the Americas. Evidence has been found that Kongo beliefs survived among slave communities in South Carolina and the Dominican Republic. Also, Catholic converts among the Kongo are thought to have played a leading role in encouraging other enslaved Africans in America to adopt Christianity.

DEATH AND THE BAKONGO

Kongo peoples believe that the creator god made the first man, Mahungu, and put him in charge of the world. Yet Mahungu soon grew lazy, sleeping most of the day and revealing God's secrets to the animals. Disappointed, God distanced himself from human affairs. Without God, Mahungu could not take care of himself and became miserable. On seeing how wretched humans were, God decided that they should be allowed to die to save them from an eternity of suffering. Thus, Kongo traditions distinguish between death by natural causes (which is a gift from God and saves humans from the frailties of old age) and premature death, which is a negative event and is believed to be caused by witchcraft.

SEE ALSO: *Christianity; Festival and ceremony; Masks and masquerade; Metalwork; Oral literature; Sculpture.*

KUBA

FACT FILE

Population	c. 250,000, all in the Democratic Republic of the Congo (DRC)
Religion	Indigenous beliefs; Christianity
Language	The Kuba language is a Central Bantu language, in the Niger-Congo language family.

TIMELINE

c.1550	Kuba migrate into the Kasai area, their present territory.
c.1600s	The Kuba kingdom becomes a regional power.
c.1800s	High point of the Kuba kingdom and its trade activity.
1885	Belgian King Leopold II founds the Congo Free State, bringing the former Kuba kingdom under his control.
1890	First Christian missions are established in Kuba territory.
1904	Kuba groups stage a failed uprising against colonial rule.
1931	The first railroad linking the Kuba territory with other areas of the Belgian Congo is opened.
1950s	Kuba play an active role in the independence struggle.
1960	Congo (Kinshasa) wins independence. Kuba separatists under Albert Kalonji form breakaway state of South Kasai.
1961	Separatists defeated and South Kasai is dissolved.
1992	Lunda peoples begin to migrate into the Kasai region, displacing significant numbers of Kuba peoples.
2005	DRC drafts new constitution in preparation for elections.

ONCE MEMBERS OF A THRIVING CENTRAL AFRICAN KINGDOM, THE KUBA WERE ABSORBED UNDER COLONIALISM INTO THE CONGO. THE KUBA COMPRISE A WIDE RANGE OF ETHNIC GROUPS.

HISTORY

The ancestors of the Kuba most likely settled in the Congo Basin during the early centuries C.E. The Kuba migrated south into the Kasai region in the mid-16th century, largely in order to take refuge from the invasions by the Jaga of the lower Congo Basin. In the 17th century the Kuba emerged as a powerful kingdom dominated by the Bushongo people, which according to Kuba oral histories was founded by Shyaam, the first king. Reaching its peak in the early 19th century, the Kuba kingdom grew prosperous from trading a variety of goods and commodities, including textiles, ivory, and slaves. The colonial era spelt an end to the prosperity of the Kuba, and during the last decade of the 19th century they were incorporated into the Congo Free State, a private colonial territory under the oppressive rule of Leopold II of Belgium.

Partly as a result of their history as a major precolonial power in Central Africa, the Kuba have always resisted efforts to reduce their independence and deprive them of self-rule. They were active in the Congolese independence struggles of the 1950s against the Belgian colonial government. At independence in 1960 many Kuba, under the leadership of Albert Kalonji (b.1929) formed a breakaway movement, which declared the region of South Kasai an independent state. However, this was quickly reincorporated into Congo (Kinshasa) by force, and later governments have attempted to quell unrest in the region by dividing it up into smaller sections.

SOCIETY AND DAILY LIFE

The Kuba are primarily a farming people, who cultivate a wide variety of crops, including cassava, corn, millet, peanuts, sweet potatoes, and beans. The Kuba have long grown cash crops for export, notably tobacco. Most farming is carried out by groups of closely related women, although heavier tasks such as clearing trees are done by men. Women and children also fish, while hunting is practiced by men. Many Kuba now live in towns and have abandoned the rural life.

A Kuba nyim. *Although the Kuba kingdom no longer exists, the office of king lives on as a ceremonial role among the Kuba.*

BWAANTSHY REGALIA

The *bwaantshy* is the official dress of the Kuba king and is worn on ceremonial and state occasions. This highly elaborate outfit comprises a red skirt woven with cowrie shells, animal skins, and various metal ornaments, including bracelets and shoulder rings. The ensemble is topped by an enormous headdress of feathers. The *bwaantshy* often weighs more than the king himself. During the ceremony, the king keeps by his side various objects symbolizing his authority, including a sword, a lance, and drums. He sits on a decorated, raised platform, which is designed to prevent the king—who is thought to be of divine descent—from touching the ground and to set him apart from his subjects.

In precolonial Kuba society, the ruling Bushongo dynasty exercised firm control through the authority of the king (*nyim*), who delegated power to local rulers. Today the Kuba kingdom no longer exists. Instead various independent chiefdoms operate in the Democratic Republic of the Congo.

Wealth and possessions are important in showing off a person's prestige and position. Kuba society is matrilineal, meaning that wealth is inherited through the female line; accordingly, a man inherits from his mother's brother, rather than from his father.

CULTURE AND RELIGION

The Kuba religion includes a belief in a supreme creator god, who is known by various names, such as Mbombo, Bumba, and Chembe. Yet although he created the world, Mbombo now has no interest in its everyday affairs. Many Kuba regard the king as having a divine status, since he is believed to be descended from Mbombo. Moreover, the creator god is thought to have given the Kuba kings the right to rule over the earth and its people.

The royal ancestor cult, although still a feature of Kuba religious practice, seems to have been more important in the past. Divination is a key feature of the Kuba religion; oracles are often consulted to determine the sources of misfortune and counteract the danger posed by sorcerers. Domestic dogs, used by the Kuba for hunting, are regarded as a powerful symbol and rubbing oracles—boards on which a diviner rubs an object and asks questions until the object moves less freely—are often made in the shape of dogs. Colonialiam and missionary activity introduced Christianity to the Kuba, yet the Kuba retain more of their preexisting religious practices than many other Central African peoples.

SEE ALSO: *Christianity; Festival and ceremony; Lunda; Masks and masquerade; Sculpture.*

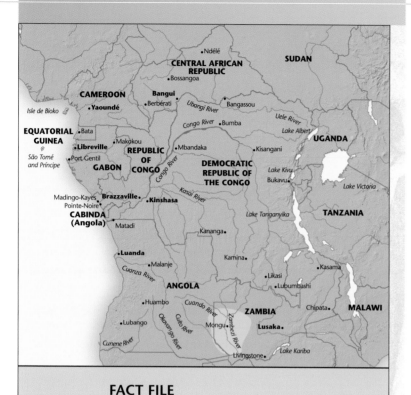

FACT FILE

Population	Over 500,000, mostly in Zambia; c.70,000 and 15,000 in Zimbabwe and Botswana respectively.
Religion	Lozi religion, Christianity
Language	The Lozi language, Kololo, is used by the Lozi royal court and includes elements of Sotho and Luyi. It is a Bantu language of the Niger-Congo language family.

TIMELINE

1600–1800	Emergence of the Lozi people in Barotseland.
1800	Mbunda and Mbalangwe migrate into east Barotseland.
1836	Kololo invaders gain control of the Barotse kingdom.
1853	British missionary David Livingstone visits Barotseland.
1864	Lozi prince Sipopo regains control of the kingdom.
1883	Paris Evangelical Mission is established in Barotseland.
1889–90	British South Africa Company (BSAC) under colonialist Cecil Rhodes gains control of Northern Rhodesia (Zambia) and negotiates a treaty with the Lozi king.
1906	Serfdom is abolished in the Lozi kingdom.
1924–25	Northern Rhodesia taken over by British government. Tribute payments to the Lozi king are abolished.
1964	Zambia wins independence from Britain.
1991	First multiparty elections held in Zambia.
2005	Drought causes severe food shortages in Zambia.

INHABITING THE CENTRAL BAROTSE PLAIN OF WESTERN ZAMBIA, WHICH IS CROSSED BY THE ZAMBEZI RIVER, THE LOZI ARE COMPOSED OF AROUND 25 ETHNIC GROUPS. TOGETHER, THEY ONCE FORMED THE BAROTSE KINGDOM.

HISTORY

The Lozi are thought to have settled in their present territory during the 17th and 18th centuries. Before the colonial era the Lozi had, by conquest and through absorbing other migrant peoples, risen to become the dominant ethnic group of the Barotse kingdom. In 1836, weakened by a period of civil war, the Lozi were overthrown by the Kololo, a Sotho-speaking group from the south. However, by 1864 a surviving Lozi prince had managed to raise an army and regain control of the Barotse kingdom.

The first Europeans to make contact with the Lozi were the Portuguese in the early 1800s. In the later 19th century the British South Africa Company annexed the region and negotiated treaties with the Lozi Kingdom. Although the Lozi lost some territory, they had great freedom to manage their own affairs, a British colonial policy known as indirect rule. Since the colonial era many neighboring peoples have migrated into the Lozi territory, including the Chokwe and the Mbunda. After Zambia became independent the Lozi kingdom still managed to keep a large degree of self-government. The region is one of the least economically developed in modern Zambia and access to transport and electricity is limited.

SOCIETY AND DAILY LIFE

The Lozi are a farming people who grow millet, cassava, corn, sorghum, peanuts, sweet potatoes, and tobacco, the latter as a cash crop. Lozi agricultural methods are

LOZI CREATION MYTHS

Nyambe, the supreme god of the Lozi, created the first man, named Kamunu, and his wife. Kamunu was clever and began to imitate Nyambe, learning from him how to make weapons from wood and metal and hunt animals. But Kamunu's ingenuity began to worry Nyambe, who feared that Kamunu might use the weapons he made against his maker. Nyambe moved to an island to try and escape from Kamunu, but the man built a canoe and followed him. Finally, Nyambe crossed a great river, climbed up a spiderweb to a place in the sky called Litooma, and blinded the spiders so they could not show Kamunu the way. Although Kamunu tried to reach Nyambe by building a high wooden platform, he failed and humankind has been separated from the Supreme God ever since.

In March or April each year, the Lozi hold a ceremony known as Kuomboka, in which the litunga *(king) leads his people in boats to find higher ground away from the flooded Zambezi River.*

quite complex. Crop-rotation, fallowing (leaving a field unfarmed for a year to allow the soil to recover), and drainage ditches are all common practices. Since the Barotse Plain floods annually from January to May, the Lozi build dams and raise mounds to protect their houses from the floodwaters. Men are mainly responsible for plowing and digging drains, while women plant, reap, and weed alongside domestic chores. The Lozi keep cattle and graze them on the plain, although only men are allowed to tend to the herds. The Lozi supplement their diet by fishing, which both men and women practice. Today, many Lozi, especially men, have quit the land to find work in towns as migrant laborers.

Lozi society has a strict hierarchy of different classes. They are ruled by a king (*litunga*), a position inherited from father to son, and a royal family. Slavery was once widespread but was abolished under colonial rule.

CULTURE AND RELIGION

Colonial missionaries brought Christianity to the Lozi, and many now attend churches. Yet others have mixed preexisting beliefs with Christianity. These include the idea of a supreme god, called Nyambe, who created the world but no longer interferes in its affairs. To strengthen their hold on power, the Lozi royal class claimed direct descent from Nyambe. Showing respect to ancestors is also a feature of Lozi religion; ancestors are the focus of most religious activities and are often asked to act as intermediaries between living people and Nyambe. The royal ancestor cult is distinct from ordinary peoples' honoring of their ancestors. In common with many other Central African societies, sorcery is seen as the main cause of misfortune and illness, and diviners are employed to find out who is using sorcery as well as to discover and fulfil the ancestors' wishes and needs.

SEE ALSO: *Christianity; Chokwe; Festival and ceremony; Masks and masquerade; Sculpture.*

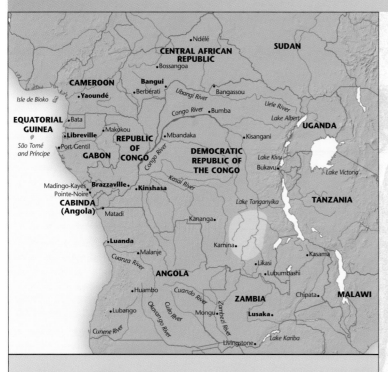

FACT FILE

Population	c.1.1 million, mainly in DRC
Religion	Preexisting beliefs; some Christianity
Language	Tshiluba, the Luba language, is a Central Bantu tongue, and part of the Niger-Congo language family.

TIMELINE

c.700	The ancestors of the Luba establish themselves in southwestern Congo (present-day DRC).
1300	The Luba are ruled by the Nkongolo, a Songye dynasty.
c.1550	Luba kingdom emerges as a centralized state.
1700s	Height of the Luba kingdom's power, extending as far east as the African Great Lakes.
1850s	Muslim Swahili of the East African coast raid the Luba.
1885	The Congo Free State is established as a private realm of King Leopold II of the Belgians.
1900	Congo Free State takes control of the Luba kingdom.
1905–17	The Luba, led by Kasongo Nyembo, fight a long war of resistance against the colonial authorities.
1960	Congo (Kinshasa) wins independence from Belgium. Katanga under Moise Tshombe breaks away from the new state. One Luba faction supports the rebels, while another, larger group fights with the government.
1965–97	Congo is ruled by the dictator Mobutu Sese Seko.
1997–2002	Mobutu is ousted in a coup, sparking a 5-year civil war.

THE LUBA LIVE IN THE SOUTHEAST OF THE DEMOCRATIC REPUBLIC OF THE CONGO, MAINLY IN THE KATANGA REGION, WITH A SMALLER NUMBER IN ZAMBIA. THEY INHABIT A WIDE RANGE OF ENVIRONMENTS, INCLUDING SAVANNA, RAINFOREST, AND ALSO MORE SWAMPY AREAS.

HISTORY

The ancestors of the Luba peoples likely first established themselves in their current territory around the eighth century, and were one of the first Central African groups to make use of iron. The Luba have a rich tradition of oral histories describing their activities over the following centuries. These suggest that the Luba kingdom emerged around the mid-16th century with the rise of the first *mulopwe* (king) Kalala Ilunga. The power of the early Luba kingdom was based on its control of regional trade in major resources, such as salt and copper.

In the 19th century the Luba had contact with the Swahili of the East African coast, who raided the kingdom for its ivory and also traded in Luba slaves. The Luba area fell under the control of Europeans by the turn of the 20th century, with the establishment of the Congo Free State by King Leopold II of the Belgians.

Under the brutal colonial regime of the Congo Free State the Luba were forced to labor in the mining and rubber industries. They rose up against colonial exploitation in 1895, and more seriously in 1905–17 under their leader Kasongo Nyembo. The rebellion was eventually defeated and its leader was forced into exile. After Congo (Kinshasa) won independence in 1960, the breakaway rebel movement that tried to establish Katanga as a separate country divided the Luba people. The central government succeeded in putting down the secession movement in 1965, leaving the pro-government Luba, under Kisula Ngoye, in a position of power in the Katanga region.

SOCIETY AND DAILY LIFE

The Luba are a farming people, who grow corn, cassava, and bananas. Millet and sorghum are also grown to brew beer. Cash crops are cultivated for export, tobacco being the most important and widely grown. The Luba mostly practice shifting cultivation —clearing new sections of forest by burning before replanting them. The Luba also fish where possible and keep a variety of domestic animals, including chickens, sheep, and pigs. Women usually carry out agricultural work and perform domestic chores, while hunting with dogs is undertaken by men. A wide range of skilled craft goods are made by the Luba, including baskets, ceramics, and netting, and these are often traded in local markets. Many Luba have also migrated to settle in towns and find employment in the mining industry, especially in Lubumbashi, the second largest city in the Democratic Republic of the Congo.

The position of king among the Luba has not existed for over a century. Although the status of local chiefs has declined in relation to central government since independence, they still play an important part in Luba society. The Luba are patrilineal, with inheritance occurring along the male line, although the opposite is true for some Luba groups. After marriage, women are generally expected to leave their family to live with their husbands and his relations, a practice that is most common in more rural areas.

RELIGION AND CULTURE

The Kuba have been subjected to some Christian influence through the missionary activity that took place under colonialism. Perhaps as a result of their long history of political self-determination and the strong resistance they put up against European rule,

ORAL HISTORIES AND THE LUBA CHIEFS

The oral histories of the Luba people tell of a tyrant called Nkongolo Muamba who once ruled over the region. A handsome and strong young hunter named Mbidi Kiluwe married the tyrant's sister, who gave birth to child named Kalala Ilunga. Kalala Ilunga proved to be a great hero, and when he had come of age he overthrew his cruel uncle and became king. The rulers of the former Luba kingdom reigned with spiritual authority as divine sovereigns. Both then and in modern times, the legend of Kalala Ilunga has played an important part in establishing the Luba chiefs' legitimacy to govern. The rulers use the myth to trace their ancestry back to the heroic founding fathers of their lineage.

they have not widely accepted Christianity. Rather, many follow preexisting religious beliefs. In common with other Bantu cultures, the Luba believe in a supreme being, Vidye, who created the world and everything in it. Spirits (*mishiki*) play an important part in day-to-day religion and are believed to regulate the natural world. Other, evil spirits are associated with sorcery and bad luck. The ancestors, who are often represented by sculptures kept in the home or worn around the neck as pendants, are also revered and must be appeased to ensure success in daily life.

SEE ALSO: *Dance and song; Festival and ceremony; Masks and masquerade; Metalwork; Oral literature; Sculpture.*

The Luba used mboko *figures such as this in divination rituals to find out the cause of illness or other problems.*

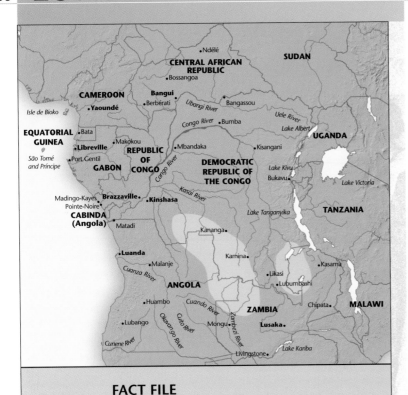

ALL OF THE MANY DIFFERENT ETHNIC GROUPS THAT ONCE COMBINED TO FORM THE POWERFUL LUNDA EMPIRE NOW COME UNDER THE BROAD HEADING *LUNDA*. THE LUNDA LIVE WIDELY ACROSS CENTRAL AFRICA.

FACT FILE

Population	c.1,500,000; 750,000 in the DRC, 490,000 in Angola, and 250,000 in Zambia
Religion	Preexisting beliefs; Christianity
Language	The Lunda language Chilunda is a Bantu tongue of the Niger-Congo family and has many dialects.

TIMELINE

c.1500	Lunda enter their present territory in the southern DRC.
c.1700	Lunda empire arises, with its capital at Musumba. The Lunda become major participants in the slave trade.
c.1800	Kazembe kingdom, a Lunda offshoot, emerges in modern Zambia, controlling key trade routes.
1885	Chokwe invade and take control of the Lunda region.
1889	Kazembe kingdom seized by British Northern Rhodesia.
1890s	The Chokwe are overthrown by the Lunda.
1904	British put Lunda of Northern Rhodesia under Lozi rule.
1950s	The Lunda political organization, CONAKAT, emerges to resist domination by colonialists, Chokwe and Luba.
1960	Congo (Kinshasa; modern DRC) wins independence. The Katanga secession led by the Lunda (CONAKAT).
1977–78	Two "Shaba wars" fought for Katangan independence.
1993	Another failed attempt is made at Katangan self-rule.
1997–2002	Civil war rages in the DRC.

HISTORY

The Lunda are thought to have been an offshoot of the neighboring Luba peoples who migrated into southern Congo in the early 16th century. By the start of the 18th century the Lunda established an empire under the rule of the *mwata yamvo* (king). This was one of the largest and most powerful states in Central African history, with a formidable army and elaborate centralized government. It controlled trade routes that spanned the whole of Central Africa. Slaves and later ivory were traded with European merchants on the Atlantic coast and Arab and Swahili merchants on the East African coast. As the Lunda expanded in the 18th and 19th centuries, allied Lunda kingdoms arose to the south and east, such as the Kazembe kingdom in what is now Zambia.

However, even before the colonial era the Lunda state had begun to break up and decline, and was invaded by neighboring peoples. The Chokwe gained control over the Lunda for a time in the late 19th century. In 1885, the Congo Free State was established in the northern Luba territory, while to the south the British began to annex Northern Rhodesia (modern Zambia), and the Portuguese occupied Angola. Like other peoples of the region, the Lunda suffered terribly under Belgian colonialism. After independence the attempted breakaway of Katanga (Shaba) province from Congo (Kinshasa) was led by Moïse Tshombe (1919–69), a Lunda royal. The Lunda have made several other attempts to win self-rule.

DAILY LIFE AND SOCIETY

The Lunda practice shifting cultivation, where tracts of forest are cleared each year for planting and left to be reclaimed by the forest after they have been exhausted. Their staple crops include corn, cassava, bananas, millet, and sorghum (the last two being used to brew beer). Domestic livestock are kept and the diet supplemented by fishing and hunting. Pineapples, corn, and cassava are grown as cash crops. Since the collapse of the Lunda empire in the late 19th century, the Lunda have not been active in long-distance trade. Yet they do engage in local commerce, especially across the border areas of Zambia, Angola, and the DRC. Some Lunda have migrated to cities, and play an important part in politics, particularly in Katanga Province.

The strict class system of the Lunda empire is still a feature of modern Lunda society. Lineages—related groups of people who, among the Lunda, trace their ancestry through the female line—play an important role. Certain lineages are accorded greater status and prestige than others. Another form of hierarchy are the age-grades, which rank individuals according to the age group to which they belong. This system helps counterbalance the structure of lineages. Chiefs still play an important role as village leaders in most areas, although their importance has declined in recent times due to increasing central government control.

Moïse Tshombe (seen here in 1960) led Katanga's attempt to break away from the Congo. This attempt failed, and Tshombe spent most of the rest of his life in exile.

CULTURE AND RELIGION

Colonialism saw Christianity become widely adopted in the Lunda territories. However, it is heavily mixed with preexisting beliefs and practices. The Lunda pray to ancestral spirits, the *akishi* (singular *mukishi*), during important ceremonies such as initiations and funerals. They also believe in a supreme being called Nzambi, who created the universe. Nzambi is not as distant from everyday human affairs as many other Central African creator gods, and may sometimes punish wrongdoers. Yet he can only be approached through the ancestors rather than directly. The Lunda see witchcraft as the cause of illnesses, and diviners are employed to find the source of evil magic.

LUNDA BIRTH-NAMES

According to one Lunda tradition, when a child is born he or she is given the same name as one of the ancestral spirits, who guides the child as he or she grows up. This is not some form of reincarnation—several children can be given the name of the same ancestor. For a baby girl, the guardian spirit is male, and vice versa for a boy. A diviner determines which spirit is to be associated with each child after the birth has taken place. Generally, the spirit is that of a paternal relative, such as the father's brother, mother, or one of his grandparents. A child's birth-name used to be a closely guarded secret in the past, but today that is not normally the case.

SEE ALSO: Chokwe; Festival and ceremony; Lozi; Luba; Marriage and the family; Sculpture.

MARRIAGE AND THE FAMILY

	Birth rate/ 1,000 population*	Deaths/ 1,000 births*	Infant mortality 1,000 births*	Children born/woman (2005 est.)	Fertility rate	HIV/AIDS in 2003 Living with (est.)	Deaths from HIV/ AIDS in 2003 (est.)
Angola	45		191		6.3	240,000	21,000
Cameroon	35		68		4.5	560,000	49,000
Central African Republic	35		91		4.5	260,000	23,000
Congo (DRC)	44		93		6.5	1.1 m	100,000
Republic of Congo	28		92		3.5	90,000	9,700
Equatorial Guinea	36		85		4.6	5,900	370
Gabon	36		54		4.8	48,000	3,000
Zambia	41		88		5.5	920,000	89,000

* per annum (2005 estimate)

CENTRAL AFRICA IS HOME TO DIVERSE MARRIAGE CUSTOMS. THE SITUATION HAS GROWN MORE COMPLEX SINCE THE COLONIAL ERA, WITH MANY DIFFERENT FORMS OF MARRIAGE EXISTING SIDE BY SIDE—FROM TRADITIONAL LOCAL PRACTICES TO CHRISTIAN WEDDINGS AND CIVIL CEREMONIES. THE POSITION OF THE FAMILY HAS ALSO UNDERGONE GREAT CHANGE.

THE ROLE OF THE FAMILY

The role and composition of the family in Central Africa have experienced major change in the face of urbanization, globalization, and conflict. The current situation is one of great diversity, with some people trying to cling to, or even restore, older family patterns, and others living in a way that more closely resembles family life in the West. The clash between "tradition" and "modernity" within the family often forms the subject of literature and films from this region, illustrating its importance and topicality in Central African culture.

A woman of the Baka people in Cameroon prepares a meal for her children. As in many traditional societies, gender roles among the Baka are clearly defined, with women gathering wild foods, practicing beekeeping, and tending children, while men hunt and trap in the forest.

Central Africa is one of the few parts of the world where matrilineal descent (with family members tracing their descent from the mother's side) is widely practiced alongside the patrilineal system (tracing descent from the father's side). A number of peoples in Central Africa, including the Ovimbundu of Angola, operate a mixture of both types. In matrilineal societies, a man usually inherits wealth and property from his uncle on his mother's side, rather than from his mother directly, since indigenous customs often prevent women from holding property in their own right.

In the more rural parts of Central Africa, a person's family still plays a vitally important role in their daily lives. In many areas a village is likely made up of people who are all related to each other. For people who have moved to the cities in search of work (an increasingly common tendency) the situation is quite different. Migration and urbanization often separate people from the rest of their kin. One of the consequences of this is that hardships can no longer be easily shared, and when food or resources are lacking it is no longer possible to rely on a family support network. The various problems that have afflicted Central Africa over the last century, including colonial

An AIDS prevention billboard in Zambia promotes fidelity as a way of combating the disease. Zambia has one of the highest rates of infection with the disease in the region.

oppression, political violence, and more recently HIV/AIDS, have taken a devastating toll on families across the region, leaving many thousands of children orphaned and lacking care.

MARRIAGE PRACTICES

Polygyny (the custom of a man having several wives) is common in Central African cultures, although it is generally only practiced by wealthier men. This is because bridewealth, either in the form of money or other valuable items, has to be paid to the bride's family to compensate them for the loss of their daughter. Women often get married in their early teens, and it is not uncommon for girls as young as 12 to be married (though this is illegal in most countries). Sharp contrasts exist between rural and urban areas of Central Africa, with city dwellers being much more likely to be monogamous and to marry at an older age. Areas where Christianity has had a major impact are also less likely to practice polygyny. Even so, it is not uncommon to find men who profess Christianity but still have more than one wife.

TRADITIONAL MARRIAGE AMONG THE LUNDA

In the past, and even to some extent today, marriage in some Central African societies was not simply about two people joining together. It also played a vital role in establishing ties between two families. Among the Lunda, for example, an older relative of a young man (say, a parent or elder brother) would give a gift such as cloth or an anklet to the parents of a girl before she reached eight years of age. If the girl's parents accepted the gift, the young man and the girl were considered to be engaged. After this, the young man himself would frequently give the girl and her parents presents and possibly also work for them. When the girl was older and had completed her initiation rites, the marriage was finalized and another gift given to her parents. The first gift payment was known as the *muivu* and had to be returned if the couple later divorced.

See also: Festival and ceremony; Lunda.

MASKING TRADITIONS OF CENTRAL AFRICA

Northwestern Central Africa

Cameroonian Grasslands	Masks are usually male, with large prominent eyes and ears and open mouths. Animals may also be represented, such as the buffalo, and may often be worn with elaborate feather costumes. Other traditions, such as those of the Kuosi, are highly abstract, with long flaps and symbolically significant patterns composed of colored beads. Abstract human figures appear in Bandjoun masks, with almond-shaped eyes and elaborate hairstyles.
Fang	Masks are often heavily stylized. Fang masks include the *ngongtang*, placed over the head with four different oval shaped faces incorporating geometric designs, and the Ngil society masks with their large, domed foreheads.
Kwele and Punu	Masks are usually stylized humans, such as the *kuk* and *mukudj* masks, which have rounded oval and concave faces, closed eyes and are decorated with geometric patterns and painted lips. Gon masks resemble gorilla skulls.

Western Congo Basin

Chokwe	*Chikunga* and *mukanda* masks are often abstract human figures, made from bark cloth and wickerwork and painted with geometric designs. They are notable for having extremely tall and elongated headdresses. Chihongo masks are made from wood and are less abstract.
Kuba	Masks are made from various materials, including copper, colored beads, wood, and shells, and are often decorated with geometric patterns. Human figures are usually depicted.
Pende	Masks are highly abstract and notable for their often large and striking goggle-shaped eyes. *Gitenga* masks are surrounded by a mane of fibers which represents the sunset.
Yaka and Suku	Masks are usually human figures with exaggerated features, such as noses and cheeks. Large bundles of raffia fibers are used to form beards and hair, as in the *kakuungu* and *mweelu* masks.

Eastern Congo Basin

Lega	Masks tend to be simple and schematic in form, pear shaped with long, thin noses and sometimes fiber beards. Faces are concave, while foreheads are bulging.
Luba	Kifwebe masks are very large and bowl shaped, decorated with rows of patterned incisions. The images are human, but abstract, with almond-shaped, closed eyes. Some Luba masks are embellished with horns.
Songye	Kifwebe masks are highly angular and abstract, often with huge squared and protruding chins and bulging eyes. Masks are decorated with colored paints.

CENTRAL AFRICAN CULTURES ARE RENOWNED FOR THEIR ELABORATE AND HIGHLY STYLIZED MASKS. THEY ARE AVIDLY COLLECTED BY LOVERS OF AFRICAN ART AND PROUDLY DISPLAYED IN MUSEUMS. YET TO THE PEOPLES WHO CREATED THEM, THESE MASKS ARE MUCH MORE THAN JUST BEAUTIFUL SCULPTURES.

When Central African masks are displayed in cabinets in Western art galleries, it is difficult to imagine the complex and dramatic rituals and ceremonies they would have played an integral part in during their "lifetime." The craftspeople who made these often skillful and attractive works of art would have been mindful of all kinds of symbolic and cultural associations when carving the masks. In fact, most Central African cultures traditionally prohibited people from looking at the masks unless they were actually being used in a performance. To realize what masks meant—and often still mean—to the Central African people who created them involves understanding their cultural context and the social roles they would have played.

MASQUERADES IN CENTRAL AFRICA

Masks form the centerpiece of one of the most important social institutions in Central Africa—the masquerade. In European and North American countries, the term *masquerade* typically refers to a large social gathering, such as a ball or party, where people arrive wearing fantastic costumes and masks. Although such occasions do have certain features in common with masquerades in Africa, the African masquerade is much more than simple entertainment.

Chokwe Pwo maskers perform at the annual festival held by the Pende at Gunga in the southern Democratic Republic of the Congo.

Masquerades in Central Africa attract large numbers of people, and often involve much music and dancing. The ceremony focuses on the movements and activities of the persons wearing the masks (maskers). Masquerades are also ritual events that are usually related to wider processes, such as the changing of the seasons, crop-planting, and harvesting, or major life events (rites of passage) such as birth, initiation, and death. The masquerade is a source of power that

CHIHONGO AND PWO

Chihongo and Pwo are two mask figures found among the Chokwe peoples of Angola and the Congo Basin. They are used today primarily in entertainments and spectacles, although they once had important ritual uses. Chihongo is male and usually appears with large eyes shaped like cowrie shells, sharpened teeth, and wearing metal earrings; he is believed to bring good fortune. His counterpart, Pwo, is a female ancestor with similar features, although she is often adorned with a headdress of pearls, colored beads, and other decorations. She is thought to encourage fertility, and represents the ideal wife. Maskers travel in groups from place to place to give performances, and both figures are worn by male maskers. Among the modern Chokwe, Pwo is being represented more and more as a young woman, reflecting a growing desire for younger women as wives in their society.

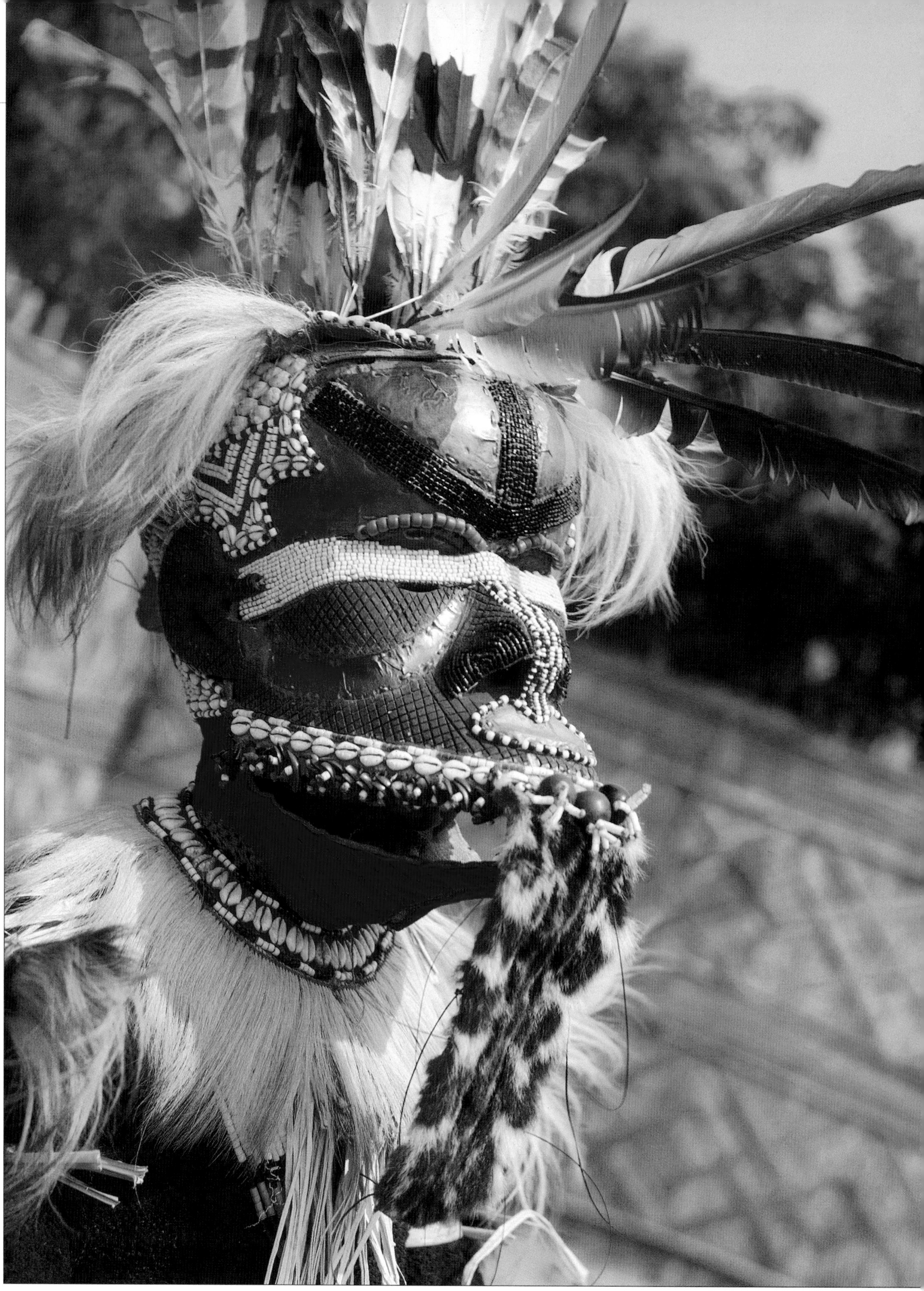

Central African peoples believe allows them to exert influence over their lives. The entire ceremony is intended to summon up a form of magic that will ensure that crops will grow or that will enable people to overcome illnesses or evil influences on their lives. Masquerades are especially important during times of change and transition, and play a vital role in successfully transforming the young into adults, allowing the old to join the ancestor spirits when they die, or marking the change in status when an individual becomes a chief.

Each mask represents a specific character, usually an ancestral or nature spirit, and has characteristic body movements and dances associated with it. For the onlookers and the participants, maskers do not act as spirits, they actually become those spirits and their own identity temporarily disappears. Indeed, few Central African cultures refer to the mask as a "mask" (and sometimes even have no word for this concept). Instead, they call the mask by the name of the spirit it represents.

Often the mask symbolizes the power and authority of the wearer. For example, the Kuba used masks called *mwaash a mbooy* as tools of royal justice. Worn by kings or chiefs, they were supposed to be able to assess people's innocence or guilt.

The ritual use of masks during initiations or at the funerals of important individuals is less widespread today than it was in precolonial times. Masks and masquerades have become increasingly associated with secular (nonreligious) occasions such as dance and cultural festivals. Many masks used in initiations were once considered sacred, and destroyed as soon as they had served their purpose. Today, they are often sold for profit as art objects or tourist items.

Made of wood, raffia textiles, cowrie shells, and beadwork, the Bwoom *mask of the Kuba appears at initiations. It is used to reenact the mythical origins of the Kuba and royal power struggles.*

THE NGIL SOCIETY OF THE FANG

Ngil is the name of an all-male secret society that once exercized considerable power in Fang society. Its members were greatly feared as legal enforcers, and would often appear at a suspect's house in the middle of the night, carrying torches, to take him away for punishment or even execution. People who were believed to be witches or sorcerers were singled out for particularly harsh treatment. The masks used by members of this society were designed to strike terror into their victims. They were made of wood that had been whitened with china clay, were often as much as 2 feet (0.6 m) high and had slit-shaped eyes and a huge, bulging forehead. The masks were commonly thought to represent the spirits of the dead and were able to protect the wearer from evil sorcery and poisons (as well as concealing his true identity). The Ngil society was disbanded by the French colonial authorities in the early 20th century.

MASKS AND SECRET SOCIETIES

Maskers are almost always male, and the masquerade is widely associated with men's societies among Central African peoples. These societies are highly secretive and closed to any uninitiated people. They operate from a society house, where the masks are usually kept. Societies were even known to possess their own secret language so they could communicate with other initiates without being understood by other members of the community. Before the establishment of colonial and postcolonial state governments, secret societies often formed an important part of the administrative apparatus of Central African kingdoms. The Ngil society of the Fang was widely feared. They served to reinforce royal authority, often acting both as judges and as the police force. Most such societies were banned by the colonial authorities and no longer exist, or at least not in the same form.

The Punu people live in Gabon, and are known for their masks representing idealized female ancestors. The diamond-shaped patterns on the mask's temples and forehead are scarification marks.

SEE ALSO: *Chokwe; Contemporary art; Dance and song; Fang; Festival and ceremony; Kuba; Mongo; Music and musical instruments; Sculpture.*

MBUTI, TWA, AND MBENGA

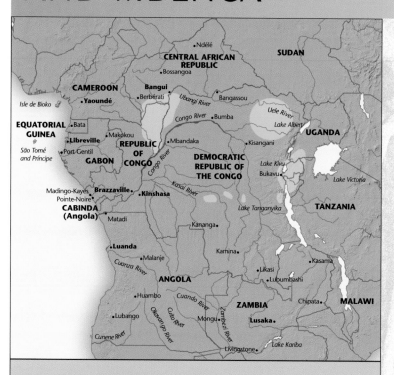

FACT FILE

Population	c.40,000 Mbuti in the DRC; 30,000 Mbenga in the Republic of Congo and Central African Republic and c.90,000 Twa in the African Great Lakes region
Religion	Preexisting beliefs
Language	The Mbuti and Twa speak dialects of Bantu, and the Mbenga dialects of Mangbetu.

TIMELINE

12,000 B.C.E.	Stone tools show presence of hunter-gatherers in Central African rainforests, including the Ituri Forest.
1000 B.C.E.–500 C.E.	Farming communities widely established throughout Central Africa.
c.1000	Hutu migrate into Twa areas (Rwanda and Burundi).
1300–1400	Tutsi herders migrate into the Twa areas.
1600 onward	Mbuti, Twa, and Mbenga take part in the ivory trade.
1880s	First direct contact with Europeans.
1964	Mbuti used as forest guides by both sides in the Simba rebellion in the Republic of Congo.
1980s	Gold-dust mining brings mass migration of outsiders and deforestation in the Ituri forest area of the Mbuti.
1994	The Rwandan genocide results in the death and displacement of many Twa.

ONCE KNOWN BY THE INSULTING TERM "PYGMIES," REFERRING TO THEIR SHORT STATURE, THE MBUTI, TWA, AND MBENGA PEOPLES ARE THOUGHT TO DESCEND FROM THE ORIGINAL INHABITANTS OF THE RAINFORESTS THAT COVER MUCH OF CENTRAL AFRICA.

HISTORY

The Mbuti live in the Ituri Forest in the northeast of the Democratic Republic of the Congo (DRC), the Mbenga (or Aka) inhabit the southwestern Central African Republic and northern Republic of Congo, and the Twa live mainly in Rwanda and Burundi, although they spill over into neighboring parts of Uganda, Tanzania, and the DRC.

The history of these peoples is hard to trace, due to the lack of written records and the problems of doing archaeology in this region, which has difficult terrain and is often politically unstable. Although migrations of Bantu-speaking farming peoples into the area from West Africa began as early as 1000 B.C.E., they did not displace the Mbuti, Twa, and Mbenga. Rather, from precolonial times, hunter-gatherer groups and agriculturalists seem to have interacted peacefully. Today, the areas inhabited by the Mbuti, Twa, and Mbenga have closely associated groups of farmers living nearby.

Also, from the start of the colonial period in the early 1500s these three peoples had indirect dealings with Europeans. From the 17th century on, they were active in the ivory trade, exchanging large quantities of elephant tusks with farmers, who sold them on to European merchants on the coast.

These peoples had little direct contact with Europeans until the late 19th century. However, once the imperial powers' "Scramble for Africa" had been formalized at the Berlin Conference on Africa in 1884–85, colonial

Mbuti people in the Ituri Forest. After preparing the bushmeat that they have helped hunt, the women usually eat in the huts with their children, while men eat in the open area at the center of the settlement.

forces encroached farther into the continent's interior. The Mbuti, Twa, and Mbenga suffered greatly, being used as forced labor in mines, on road building, and to tap rubber. The colonial administration in the Congo Free State established as the personal realm of the Belgian King Leopold II was especially brutal. After independence these peoples have continued to face difficulties, since there were fewer of them and they were less powerful than their farming neighbors. Since the 1970s they have suffered government resettlement programs, expulsion from their traditional hunting lands, and the ravages of war.

THE TWA AND THE RWANDAN GENOCIDE

In 1994 ethnic conflict between the Hutu and Tutsi peoples of Rwanda killed almost 1 million people, most of them Tutsi. The Twa also suffered greatly, but because they make up less than 1 percent of the Rwandan population their plight did not receive nearly as much international attention. It is estimated that some 10,000 Twa were killed, while a similar number fled to neighboring countries. Many Twa have been left orphaned or widowed and are very vulnerable to disease and poverty. The Twa have found it especially difficult to maintain their way of life, with many resorting to begging or farm laboring to survive.

SOCIETY AND DAILY LIFE

The Mbuti, Twa, and Mbenga are generally shorter than other human populations, with an average height of just 4 feet and 9 inches (1.45 m). Their stature comes from their habitat, where tallness would make it hard to move around the rainforest when hunting. They mainly hunt duikers (small deerlike animals) with nets. Bushpigs, buffaloes, elephants, and monkeys are killed with spears or arrows. Men and women hunt together, with the women beating the undergrowth to drive animals into nets held by the men.

Cultivated and wild plants supplement their diet. During the rainy season, people live in small, semipermanent camps of related individuals near farming villages. The villagers exchange crops for forest products such as honey and bushmeat, and the Mbuti, Twa, and Mbenga may also sell their labor to the villagers. In the dry season they move to temporary camps farther away from the farming areas. Their hunter-gatherer lifestyle is under growing threat; deforestation since the 1960s has forced many of these peoples to become wage laborers or forest guides.

CULTURE AND RELIGION

The forest holds the central place in the belief systems of these peoples. It is seen as a great womb from which all people come, and to which they return when they die. It is also the home of the spirits of the ancestors, who must be appeased through dancing and ritual. Masks are a key part of these rituals, representing the most important supernatural beings such as the "Spirit of the Elephant." Most Mbuti, Twa, and Mbenga also believe in creator gods and other powerful beings, such as Apakumandua, the Mbuti "Father of the Forest." Nganga are persons who act as divine healers, having the ability to link the mortal and spirit worlds.

SEE ALSO: *Festival and ceremony; Masks and masquerade; Mongo; Oral literature; Textiles.*

METALWORK

METALWORKING WAS FIRST PRACTICED IN CENTRAL AFRICA IN AROUND THE FIFTH CENTURY B.C.E. IRON AND COPPER SOON BECAME ASSOCIATED WITH POWER, AND IMPORTANT STATES DEVELOPED IN AREAS WITH MAJOR DEPOSITS OF METAL ORES. NUMEROUS WEAPONS, FARMING IMPLEMENTS, AND CEREMONIAL OBJECTS IN METAL HAVE BEEN FOUND AT ARCHAEOLOGICAL SITES ACROSS THE REGION.

In ancient times the technology required to produce metals from their ores was unknown to humans. Tools such as harpoons, spears, and knives were made from flints (chipped stones) or by carving animal bones, while jewelry and other decorative items consisted of colored beads and shells, often as part of necklaces. This era is known as the Later Stone Age in Africa. The processes of metal production emerged in areas south of the Sahara during the 1st millennium B.C.E. and spread rapidly across the continent over the following centuries, heralding the onset of the Iron Age. In other parts of the world, particularly Europe and Asia, a Bronze Age, in which copper and its alloys were known but iron was not, comes before the Iron Age. For reasons that are unclear, there was no Bronze Age in sub-Saharan Africa and so the Iron Age follows on immediately from the Later Stone Age.

Copper is a vital export commodity for some Central African countries, such as the Democratic Republic of the Congo (seen here, the copper mines at Katanga in the southern DRC) and Zambia.

BEGINNINGS OF METALWORKING

Iron smelting appears to have spread into Central Africa at the same time as the expansion of people in the region speaking Bantu languages. It was probably introduced from either West Africa or the African Great Lakes region. The earliest archaeological sites with evidence of metal production date to around the fifth century B.C.E. and are concentrated in the north in modern Gabon and Cameroon. There followed a gradual expansion of metalworking technology southward and along the river systems of the Congo Basin. However, metalworking was not adopted right across Central Africa at this time, and there is evidence of peoples using only stone technologies in some areas, including the Ubangi Valley, up until 400 C.E. The use of copper and its alloys seems to have begun around the same as the appearance of iron smelting.

The introduction of metalworking to Central African cultures had several highly significant effects. The most obvious were improvements in weaponry and agricultural tools. Metal spears or farming axes are far more effective than their stone

The Bakota people of Gabon made mbulu-ngulu *figures from wood covered with copper sheeting. They were used to guard reliquary baskets containing the bones of important ancestors.*

wealth in metal form. Areas where high-quality iron ores were plentiful became the centers of important chiefdoms. Metals also stimulated trade between neighboring areas.

METALWORK AND SOCIETY

Copper collars are common status objects in Central African cultures. In Cameroon, chiefs would give warriors collars decorated with metal buffalo heads to reward them for courageous feats. Today they are also worn by elders at important meetings. Some collars can weigh up to 12 pounds (5.5 kg); the larger the collar, the greater the prestige of the person wearing it. Similar objects are often worn by women as anklets. Among the Fang these traditionally form part of a women's dowry, the share of her own family's wealth that is paid to her when she marries.

Metallic objects often have ceremonial functions and act as symbols of individual authority. The chiefs of the Suku and Yaka peoples, for example, carry ceremonial weapons of forged iron called *khaamdu* over their left shoulders as a sign of their status. Similarly, the Luba kings used to wear axes made of wrought iron and copper, decorated with sculpted human figures.

SEE ALSO: Fang; Festival and ceremony; Luba; Marriage and the family; Masks and masquerade; Mongo; Sculpture.

equivalents for harvesting crops, tilling fields, or waging war. Yet the social consequences of metalworking were even more important than the technological changes it brought. Iron and copper were the "precious metals" of sub-Saharan Africa, and were used to make jewelry, coinage, and other high-value items. The power and prestige of chiefs and kings often depended on their ability to control and accumulate

RIGOBERT NIMI

Rigobert Nimi (b.1965) is a contemporary sculptor from the Democratic Republic of the Congo, who uses machined metal and engineering components to create futuristic works of art. These often take the form of space vessels or robot factories. He become known internationally in 2005, when his work was shown at the African Art Now exhibiting at the Museum of Fine Arts in Houston, Texas. Nimi's sculptures are large and meticulously constructed; it often takes him well over a year to make each one. The sculptures are crafted from a variety of materials including iron, steel, aluminum, copper, electrical equipment, and plastics, and are working machines with moving parts. Rigobert Nimi's best-known works include *Venus* (2001) and *Usine Robotisée* (2003).

MONGO

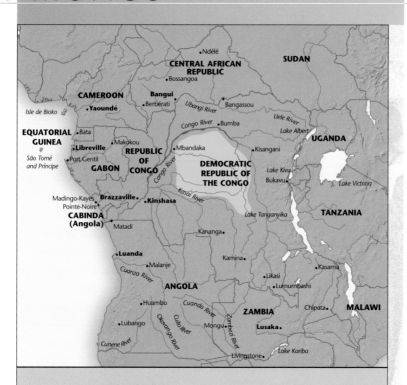

FACT FILE

Population	Approximately 3.5 million, all in the DRC
Religion	Christianity; preexisting beliefs
Language	The Mongo language, with many related dialects, is part of the Bantu branch of the Niger-Congo language family.

TIMELINE

c.100 Bantu-speaking groups established in their present area.

c.1000 The Mongo adopt banana cultivation.

1885 Congo Free State founded by Belgian King Leopold II.

1892–1910 Rubber trade booms in the Congo Free State.

1908 Belgian government takes control of the Congo Free State, which is renamed the Belgian Congo.

1933 The Belgian authorities introduce their economic development plan for the Congo, increasing the number of plantations and exports. The authority of Mongo chiefs is officially recognized.

1960 Congo (Kinshasa) wins independence from Belgium.

1965 Mobutu Sese Seko seizes power in a coup in Congo.

1971 Congo (Kinshasa) renamed Zaïre.

1997–2001 Mobutu is ousted by Laurent Kabila. A long period of civil war ensues until Kabila is assassinated.

2002–03 Foreign forces withdraw from the Democratic Republic of the Congo and an interim government is established.

T HE MONGO ARE BANTU PEOPLES INHABITING THE RAINFORESTS OF THE CONGO BASIN, IN THE NORTHWEST OF THE DEMOCRATIC REPUBLIC OF THE CONGO.

HISTORY

The Mongo are the descendants of Bantu speakers who probably migrated into the Congo Basin from around 200 B.C.E. They grew yams at first but later switched to bananas, which remain their staple diet. The inhospitable nature of their rainforest home shielded them from European encroachment until the late 19th century, when the colonial powers began to venture inland from their coastal enclaves. From the 1870s the Mongo, particularly those living along navigable rivers, supplied the Europeans with ivory, which they bought from neighboring peoples such as the Twa. The Mongo, who were well placed to control the main trade routes, profited enormously from this trade.

A chief at a 1950s ceremony near Lac Mai-Ndombe in the Belgian Congo (present-day DRC). This lake was formerly named Lake Leopold II for the Belgian king who imposed his tyrannical rule on this region in the late 19th century.

From the 1890s, the Mongo were subjected to brutal repression by the Congo Free State, a private colonial possession of Belgium's King Leopold II (see box feature). The Belgian state was forced to take control of the Free State in 1908, which brought some improvements for the Mongo and other Congolese peoples. By the 1920s the Mongo were even allowed to profit from producing their own rubber and ivory. Yet the Great Depression in the 1930s saw forced labor and cash-crop plantations reintroduced to Mongo areas. As a result, anticolonial resistance movements arose, such as the Likili. However, Congo (Kinshasa) did not win its independence until 1960.

SOCIETY AND DAILY LIFE

In precolonial times the Mongo practiced shifting (or slash-and-burn) cultivation of bananas, oil palms, cassava, and corn. Crop-growing was combined with hunting, fishing, and foraging wild foods from the forest, such as wild fruits, seeds, insects, and mushrooms. Although these food sources are still exploited in a limited way by the Mongo today, agriculture has become more important, especially the production of cash crops such as coffee and cocoa for the export market. Women generally do most of the agricultural work, wild-food foraging, and fishing, while men hunt larger animals, such as antelope, and trap smaller prey.

The Mongo never formed a unified political group or kingdom. Until Belgian colonial rule was imposed on them, they recognized few authorities outside their local village. In Mongo society, power is generally held by men, and wealth and status are inherited from father to son. Women are expected to move in with their husband's family after marriage. Each village has a headman (*bokulaka*), together with a council

The Tetela, a Mongo subgroup, use mwadi *masks such as this in marriage and funeral ceremonies.*

of senior men, who make decisions on matters affecting the whole community. In the past, Mongo society also had a class of slaves who had been captured in raids on neighboring peoples. Over time, the slaves and their descendants were absorbed into Mongo society.

CULTURE AND RELIGION

Mongo religion has many similarities with those of other Bantu-speaking peoples of Central Africa. Nature spirits, which are thought to play a key role in ensuring fertility, are the focus of day-to-day religious activity, along with the ancestral spirits of the dead. A supreme god, Nzakomba, is believed to have created the first people as well as the earth and sky. Belief in witchcraft, and the use of diviners to combat the effects of sorcery, are widespread.

Since the late 19th century, Roman Catholic missionaries from Belgium and Protestant missionaries from Britain and the United States have been active in spreading Christianity among the Mongo. However, many Mongo Christians now intermingle preexisting and Christian beliefs and practices.

SEE ALSO: *Christianity; Masks and masquerade; Mbuti, Twa, and Mbenga; Metalwork.*

THE "CONGO FREE STATE" OF KING LEOPOLD II

The vast area now occupied by the Democratic Republic of the Congo was once ruled as a private colony by the Belgian King Leopold II (1835–1909). The king financed explorations in the region in the 1870s, notably by the U.S. explorer Henry Morton Stanley, and was keen to acquire a foreign colony to boost Belgian prestige. Leopold succeeded in having his claims to sovereignty over the "Congo Free State" recognized by other European governments at the Berlin Conference on Africa in 1884–85. Leopold's Free State regime soon became notorious for its mistreatment of the African population. The rubber trade, in which forced laborers had to meet unrealistically high quotas or suffer brutal punishment, hit the Mongo especially hard. International outrage at these abuses, which are thought to have caused the death of up to 6 million people, forced the Belgian government to take control of the Congo Free State in 1908.

CENTRAL AFRICAN MOVIES AND MOVIEMAKERS

Title	Date	Director	Country
Faz la Coragen Camarada! (Courage, Comrade!)	1977	Rui Duarte de Caralho	Angola
Nelista	1983	Rui Duarte de Caralho	Angola
La Vie est Belle (Life is Rosy)	1986	Mweze Ngangura & Benoit Lavy	DRC
Les Messages des Îles (Messages from the Islands)	1989	Rui Duarte de Caralho	Angola
La Chapelle (The Chapel)	1989	Jean-Michel Tschissoukou	Republic of the Congo
Sango Malo (The Village Teacher)	1991	Bassek ba Kobhio	Cameroon
Quartier Mozart (Mozart Quarter)	1992	Jean-Pierre Bekolo	Cameroon
Africa, je te plumerai (Africa, I Will Fleece You)	1992	Jean-Marie Teno	Cameroon
La Tête dans les Nuages (Head in the Clouds)	1994	Jean-Marie Teno	Cameroon
Pièces d'Identités (Pieces of Identity)	1998	Mweze Ngangura	Republic of the Congo
Dôlé (Money)	2001	Imunga Ivanga	Gabon
O Heroi (The Hero)	2005	Zézé Gamboa	Angola
Les Habits Neufs du Gouverneur (The Governor's New Clothes)	2005	Mweze Ngangura	Republic of the Congo

MANY INTERESTING AND DIVERSE CENTRAL AFRICAN MOVIES HAVE BEEN PRODUCED OVER THE LAST FEW DECADES. HOWEVER, THE REGION'S FILM INDUSTRY CONTINUES TO FACE MANY PROBLEMS, INCLUDING A CHRONIC LACK OF FUNDING AND THE DIFFICULTY OF DECIDING WHETHER TO MAKE MOVIES IN AFRICAN OR EUROPEAN LANGUAGES.

THE DEVELOPMENT OF CINEMA IN CENTRAL AFRICA

The earliest films in Central Africa were made at the instigation of the European powers then controlling the region. In 1943 the colonial authorities of French Equatorial Africa established a service to distribute movies, mainly documentaries, to Africans within their colonial territory. Innovations such as mobile cinema-buses were introduced to show movies to rural populations who would otherwise not have had access to movie theaters. The Belgian Ministry of Information soon developed similar organizations in the Belgian Congo, notably the missionary-led *Centre Congolais Catholique d'Action Cinématographique*. However, these initiatives often took a superior and patronizing attitude toward

ÉCRANS NOIRS FILM FESTIVAL

The *Écrans Noirs* (Black Screens) festival is one of Central Africa's most prominent film events. It takes place in Yaoundé, Cameroon, for one week in June every year. The purpose of the festival is to promote and show French-language movies by African directors from across Central Africa. The organization is active in providing information about African cinema in several countries, including Cameroon, Gabon, Central African Republic, and the two Congo republics. Since the founding of the *Écrans Noirs* in 1995, 80 different films have been shown. In 2003 a program was insituted to set up large public screens in schools and rural areas to reach a wider audience. Although it is primarily devoted to African cinema, *Écrans Noirs* has shown some European films as well, in order to increase awareness of European cinema among African audiences.

their African audiences. The Belgian authorities, for example, refused to show European or U.S. movies to Black Africans, since they believed that Africans were not "mature" enough to understand feature films, and that a quick succession of images and complex plot lines would confuse and upset them.

The colonial powers refused to sponsor the production of films that expressed any negative or critical views of European influence in Africa, however mildly. In the postcolonial era, Africans were more free to make movies with themes that were truly relevant to their everyday life and addressed their concerns. In 1970 the Pan-African Cinema Federation was created to promote the development of African films and distribute movies by African directors. In general, French-speaking countries in Central Africa (as in West Africa) have the most fully developed film industries. This is a direct result of French government policies, which encouraged and funded cultural development even after independence. More recently, the European Union has invested U.S.$6 million in Central African moviemaking since 2000.

The earliest homegrown movies from the 1950s and 1960s such as *La Grande Case* (1951) and *Kalla* (1955), both made in Cameroon, focused on the histories and cultures of African peoples. Feature films later followed. A major theme of movies from the postindependence period has been the tension between the "traditional" and "modern" worlds in Africa. The Congolese film *La Vie est Belle* tells the story of a poor rural musician whose flute is accidentally broken, prompting him to move to the capital Kinshasa, where he finds success playing modern electrical instruments. *La Chapelle* portrays the clash between a village sorcerer and a French schoolteacher and the eventual triumph of African wisdom and values over those of Europeans. Imunga Ivanga's *Dôlé* treats the theme of poverty and crime, telling how a gang of street kids in Libreville plan a raid on a lottery booth to pay for the gang leader's mother's urgent medical treatment.

Documentary film-making from and about the Central African region is stimulated by many newsworthy events there. Here, a French director is making a documentary on ivory poaching in the Democratic Republic of the Congo (then Zaïre) in 1989.

SEE ALSO: *Contemporary art; French-language literature; Television and radio.*

MAJOR STYLES AND KEY PERFORMERS

Style	Artist/Group	Country
Afroma	New Scene	Zambia
Bikutsi	Los Camaroes	Cameroon
Kalindula	Junior Mulemena Bamd	Zambia
Kilapanda	Afra Sound Star	Angola
Kizomba	Prenda Boys Band	Angola
Makossa	Manu Dibango Ekambi Brilliant Papa Zoé	Cameroon
Congolese Rumba (Soukous)	Kanda Bongo Man African Jazz Franco's OK Jazz	DRC
Rumba-Rock	Zaiko Langa Langa	DRC
Semba	Bonga	Angola
Zam-Rock	Musi-o-tunya Great Witch	Zambia

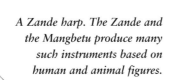

A Zande harp. The Zande and the Mangbetu produce many such instruments based on human and animal figures.

THE CULTURAL DIVERSITY OF CENTRAL AFRICA IS REFLECTED IN THE VARIETY OF ITS MUSICAL FORMS. MUSICIANS FROM THE REGION HAVE ABSORBED A WIDE RANGE OF INFLUENCES FROM ACROSS THE AFRICAN CONTINENT AND BEYOND, MOST NOTABLY PORTUGAL AND LATIN AMERICA.

TRADITIONAL MUSIC

Music in Central Africa did not remain static and unchanging for thousands of years during the region's precolonial history. Archaeological finds provide clues which indicate that changes took place in the styles of music played, in the purposes for which it was played, and in the types of instruments used. For example, iron bells dating to around 800 C.E. have been excavated from Katanga Province in the south of the Democratic Republic of the Congo. Yet such

HARPS OF THE ZANDE AND MANGBETU

The Mangbetu and Zande cultures are known for producing exquisitely decorated harps. These objects are as much pieces of visual art as they are musical instruments, and were eagerly collected by Europeans in the 20th century. Some are so ornate that playing them would have been difficult; accordingly, musical scholars have concluded that their main purpose was display. Made from wood and sometimes other unusual materials, such as the scales of the pangolin (an African ant-eating mammal), the harps have five strings stretched between a neck and a resonator. They may incorporate carvings, with elaborately hairstyled heads, arms, and legs and incised lines representing body-painting patterns that were once fashionable among Mangbetu women. The harps were generally used by individual performers to provide entertainment, rather than in royal court settings.

hard-and-fast evidence is rare. Unfortunately, other ancient musical instruments made from more perishable materials. such as wood or animal hide, have long since disintegrated in the humid tropical rainforest environment. Where more recent centuries are concerned, written historical accounts that have survived provide a better picture of how musical practices and cultures have changed over time.

A number of key musical innovations from the last four hundred years have been documented showing the dynamic nature of Central African music. In the 17th and 18th centuries, iron-key lamellaphones (mbira) from the Zambezi Valley were adopted by many cultures, including the Lunda. Increased long-distance contacts as a result of the growing slave and ivory trade in the 19th century also saw new instruments being imported from other parts of the continent. These included the zither, which was introduced to Zambia and the Congo from East Africa. Central Africa was also responsible for creating its own innovations, such as box-resonated lamellaphones, which were invented in the lower Congo in the mid-19th century and later spread to groups such as the Baya and the Zande.

CHRISTIAN INFLUENCES

Christian music was first brought to the Kongo kingdom by Portuguese missionaries in the late 1400s. Church bells were a popular introduction, and inspired the manufacture of small clapper bells by the Kongo for use in their musical ceremonies. The spread of Christianity was given a new lease of life and greatly extended by colonial administrations in the 19th and 20th centuries. Since the 1950s some areas have been active in developing their own forms of Christian worship and music that incorporate both European and African elements.

MODERN GENRES: POPULAR AND URBAN MUSIC

Since the 1940s the influx into the region of Western instruments such as the guitar, the saxophone, and, more recently, the electric guitar, has stimulated several vibrant modern musical styles. Kinshasa and Brazzaville in particular have been major centers in the development of the Congolese rumba and have produced a number of internationally famous guitar-based ensembles such as the OK Jazz Band, Les Bantous, and African Jazz. The music of Latin America and the Caribbean has had the greatest effect on such groups, with Cuban singer–songwriters such as Guillermo Portobales being regarded as major influences.

Congolese rumba, which is usually performed in French or Lingala, has become the mainstay of the music industry throughout sub-Saharan Africa. Produced for a mass-market audience, it has given rise to several

This wooden carving made by the Chokwe people of Angola shows a chief playing a sanza. This type of instrument, also known as a mbira, is a lamellaphone plucked with the thumbs to produce a gentle, ringing sound. It is played widely in sub-Saharan Africa.

superstars, mainly from the DRC, such as Kanda Bongo Man (b.1955).

Although Congolese output dominates the popular music of Central Africa, other strong traditions exist elsewhere. These include the guitar-and-drums "Zam-Rock" of Zambia and the fast, bouncy dance music from Cameroon known as Makossa. The Makossa artist Manu Dibango (b.1933), who plays the saxophone and keyboards, achieved international success with the Disco hit *Soul Makossa*, which made the U.S. Top 40 in 1973. Since then, Central African music has become increasingly well-known abroad, especially as a result of the "world music" boom in the 1980s and 1990s.

See also: Dance and song; Festival and ceremony; Masks and masquerade; Zande.

Chokwe drummers and xylophone (marimba) players. Drums in Central Africa come in a range of forms and sizes. The many types include the kettledrum, the slit drum, and the talking drum.

FRANCO LUAMBO MAKIADI

The Congolese guitarist Franco Luambo Makiadi, born in Kinshasa in 1938, was one of Central Africa's most renowned popular musicians. He made his first guitar himself from a tin can and recycled electrical wiring, and by the age of 15 had already become a celebrity, attracting a devoted following of female fans. In 1956 he became a founder-member of the OK Jazz, perhaps the most famous band to have emerged from Central Africa. Often called the "Sorcerer of the Guitar" for his skillful playing, Franco was responsible for blending African rhythms with the Congolese rumba in a style that became known as soukous. Makiadi often used his music to put across social messages, particularly regarding the dangers of HIV/AIDS. During his career he released over 150 albums, and when he died in 1989 a period of national mourning was declared.

NGBANDI

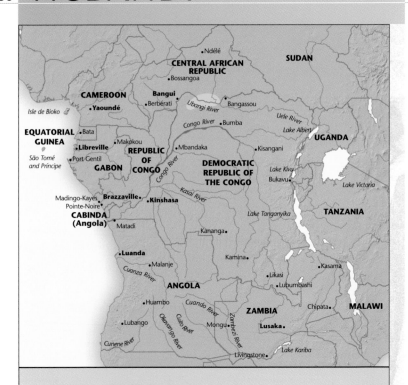

FACT FILE
Population	200,000, mainly in the DRC
Religion	Christianity; preexisting beliefs
Language	The Ngbandi language is an Adamawa-Ubangi tongue, and is part of the wider Niger-Congo language family.

TIMELINE

c.1500	The ancestors of the Ngbandi settle in the area between the Ubangi and Congo rivers.
1880s	The French make contact with the Ngbandi, who act as middlemen for trade in the region.
1885	Belgian King Leopold II founds the Congo Free State
1890	The Banziri, a Ngbandi subgroup, conclude a protection treaty with the French.
1894	Province of Ubangi-Shari (modern Central African Republic) is incorporated into French Equatorial Africa.
1960	The Belgian Congo achieves independence.
1965	Mobutu Sese Seko, a Ngbandi, seizes power in Congo.
1981	Laurent Kolingba, a Ngbandi, emerges as ruler of the Central African Republic.
1993	Kolingba is deposed as Central African Republic leader.
1997	Mobutu is ousted by Laurent Kabila.
1993–2003	Kolingba's successor in the Central African Republic, Ange-Félix Patasse, persecutes the Ngbandi.

THE NGBANDI LIVE MAINLY ALONG THE UBANGI RIVER IN EQUATEUR PROVINCE IN THE NORTHWEST OF THE DEMOCRATIC REPUBLIC OF THE CONGO. A SMALL NGBANDI POPULATION ALSO LIVES IN THE CENTRAL AFRICAN REPUBLIC.

HISTORY

The Ngbandi are made up of several related peoples, all of whom are believed to have migrated into their present territory in the Congo-Ubangi region sometime during the 16th century. It is believed that their original home was in the Upper Nile region of what is now southern Sudan. Before the colonial era, the Ngbandi played a major role as boatmen and traders. With the arrival of the first Europeans in their region in the 19th century, they acted as middlemen, selling goods on to the French that they bought from peoples living deeper in the Central African interior. The northern Ngbandi (in the present-day Central African Republic) were incorporated into French Equatorial Africa in 1894, while the Congo Free State of the Belgian King Leopold II had extended its influence into the Congo-Ubangi region by the end of the 19th century.

After independence the Ngbandi gained a political influence that was out of proportion to their relatively small numbers. They occupied prominent positions in the government and police of both the Central African Republic and Congo (Kinshasa). Mobutu Sese Seko, who ruled Congo (later Zaïre, now the DRC) from 1965 until 1997, was of Ngbandi origin and promoted many of his fellow people to his bodyguard, the Special Presidential Division. In the Central African Republic, Laurent Kolingba, who ruled from 1981 until 1993, was a Yakoma, a subgroup of the Ngbandi, and also appointed many of his own people to important government positions. Since the fall of Mobutu and Kolingba in the 1990s, the Ngbandi have lost much of their special status. In the Central African Republic they suffered violent reprisals after the fall of Kolingba.

SOCIETY AND DAILY LIFE

The Ngbandi are principally a farming people, although fishing still supplies an important part of their daily diet. Farming is generally conducted using shifting cultivation techniques, with sections of forest and bush being cleared for planting through fire. The main crops are corn, sorghum, manioc, and bananas. Beer fermented from sorghum and corn is also drunk. Ngbandi villages are small and widely dispersed throughout their territory. Many Ngbandi also play a major part in local trading networks, using the rivers as a means of transport. Men are generally responsible for the clearing sections of the forest ready for planting. The remainder of the agricultural work, such as sowing and harvesting, is carried out by women and children.

The Ngbandi had little or no history of large-scale organization or centralized government before the colonial era. Each village is made up of an extended family or clan. The village headman is customarily the most senior member of the family unit and has several responsibilities, including the administration of justice. For the most part, the Ngbandi are a patrilineal people, who

A Ngbandi cup from the Ubangi River region, carved in the form of a large human head set on stout legs. This sculpture is made of hardwood, with brass stud decoration.

trace their relationships and inheritance rights through the male line, from father to son. However, relationships through the female line are not ignored and people also consider them important.

CULTURE AND RELIGION

The religion of the Ngbandi is mainly focussed on the ancestors (*toro*), who are regularly provided with offerings to ensure that they will help and favor the living in their day-to-day activities. For the Ngbandi, the relationship between the living and the dead is very much one of exchange and mutual dependency. The Ngbandi also recognize the existence of a supreme creator god, whom they call Nzapa. He is regarded as the source of all life and is specifically linked with female fertility, although he is never worshipped directly.

Powerful spirits, who were created by Nzapa and are regarded as distinct from the ancestor spirits, also play an important role in Ngbandi religion. These spirits are often associated with nature, and individual families may often hold a specific spirit in special reverence, which they believe acts as their guardian. People regularly bring ritual offerings to shrines to appease these spirits.

There is also a widespread belief among the Ngbandi in magic and sorcerers, known as *kokoro*, and diviners, called *bendo*. Although European missionaries only arrived relatively late in Ngbandi territory, many people have accepted Christianity today, and practice a mixture of Christian and preexisting beliefs.

SEE ALSO: *Christianity; Dance and song; Festival and ceremony; Masks and masquerade; Oral literature; Sculpture.*

EXAMPLES OF ORAL LITERATURE

All Central African peoples have **creation myths**. The Bashongo (a subgroup of the Luba) believe that a supreme being called Bumba had a stomachache and, feeling sick, vomited up first the sun, then the moon, and a number of animals, including the leopard, crocodile, and turtle. One of the last creatures to come out was a human being; as a result, the Bashongo do not believe that humans are any more important than other living beings. Another creation legend, told by the Mbuti of the Ituri Forest, has many similarities to the Christian Garden of Eden in the Old Testament; the Mbuti regard their rainforest habitat as central to their existence and see its natural riches as a form of paradise.

Many **trickster myths** in Central Africa tell of weak, small animals outwitting bigger, stronger ones. The Zande have a story of Ture the spider, who one day met a monster who was in the habit of trapping and killing people inside a huge, double-sided gong that he carried with him. Ture asked the monster to show him how he did it; as the monster climbed inside his own gong, Ture slammed the lid shut, killing him.

The Fang have an **epic storytelling tradition** that they call *mvet*. These tales revolve around wars between the men of the Oku Clan and their immortal enemies, the Engong, who are ruled by a Great Man of Power called Akoma Mba. The characters in these struggles often demonstrate fantastic magical powers, such as the ability to fly. One of the most famous Central African epics is the tale of Mwindo. This legend is widespread throughout the region, but is particularly associated with the Nyanga people of the eastern Democratic Republic of Congo. It tells the story of a master hunter who has a miraculous birth. Mwindo's travels take him down into the underworld and up into the sky, and he is given special powers. When he begins his epic journey he is a strong, confident, but boastful young man. In the course of his adventures, he learns the virtues of modesty and reason, and finally becomes a greatly revered leader of the Nyanga.

ORAL LITERATURE OF THE NGBANDI

The Ngbandi have a long tradition of telling stories and proverbs. These are collectively called *mvene* ("spider," reflecting their complex interwoven nature, like a spiderweb). Many Ngbandi stories revolve around small animals, such as birds, mice, and small antelope, who encounter larger and more powerful animals like the leopard and always succeed in outsmarting them. One of the most important characters is Tiya, who embodies wisdom and forethought and is regarded as a diviner. Another mythological figure in Ngbandi oral traditions is called Mvene, a cunning and clever figure who always plays the role of the trickster. The stories of the Ngbandi commonly teach a moral lesson relating to some aspect of social behavior.

ORAL LITERATURE IN CENTRAL AFRICA IS A COMMUNAL ACTIVITY THAT TAKES PLACE IN PUBLIC. OFTEN THE AUDIENCE IS ENCOURAGED TO PARTICIPATE. PERFORMANCES CAN BE VERY LONG, SOMETIMES LASTING FOR SEVERAL DAYS AT A TIME.

In Central Africa, performers of oral literature are often initiates into spirit cults, for whom storytelling is a part of their profession. Performers are introduced to their art by apprenticeships under more experienced storytellers, unlike some other regions in Africa where performers are a specific social group that a person must be born into. Storytelling is usually undertaken by men, although women have occasionally been known to perform as well.

PERFORMERS AND AUDIENCES

Generally speaking, there is a lead performer, who is supported by a backing chorus that sings and plays music. There is no strict division between the audience and the storytellers, and those who are listening may also join in the songs and dances that are interspersed throughout the tale. The lead performer passionately acts out the events as he describes them.

Oral literature may take a number of forms, including poetry, history, myth, and epics. Often these various forms overlap. Epic literature is particularly common in Central Africa. There is not a strict historical dimension to the stories, which take place in a timeless and mythical reality. Unlike in written literature, oral stories change with each performance, with new elements being added or old ones taken away. The storyteller creates as he performs, with each performance generating a unique piece of art through improvization. Stories, often

In Africa, when oral literature is performed, it almost always incorporates other art forms such as music, dancing, and song. The Pende regularly hold a festival called the Mbuya, which involves as many as 20 different characters from folklore. This stilt dancer is portraying N'Tomo, a good-natured spirit who lives in the trees and protects young people.

narrated by animal characters, focus on famous heroic figures, such as Mwindo.

One of the most famous types of animal legend in the Central African storytelling tradition is the trickster myth. The Bantu-speaking peoples of the region all have legends concerning the cunning hare, who outwits larger jungle animals. In one well-known tale, hare plans to get married. Being too lazy to make the necessary preparations to set up a home for his future wife, he sets out to find dupes to do the work for him. He first encounters the hippopotamus, whom he asks to hold one end of a long rope, and then the elephant, whom he persuades to hold the other. These large, powerful animals cannot see each other, and start a fierce tug-of-war that brings down trees and clears all the undergrowth between them. Hare then moves in on the land they have unwittingly prepared for him. The wily Brer Rabbit figure in the "Uncle Remus" tales told by African slaves in America has his origins in African folklore.

Although storytelling is now becoming less common in Central Africa, its influence is still seen in many novels and movies.

SEE ALSO: African-language literature; Baya; Dance and song; Fang; Festival and ceremony; Kongo; Lozi; Luba; Masks and masquerade; Movies; Pende; Zande.

OVIMBUNDU

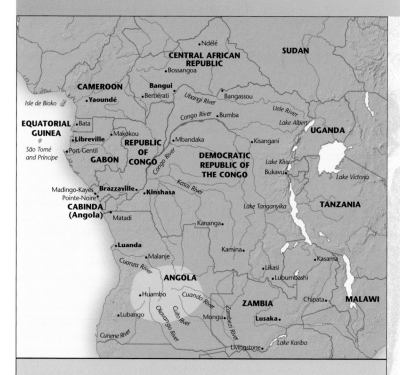

FACT FILE

Population	4,000,000 in Angola
Religion	Preexisting beliefs; Christianity
Language	The Ovimbundu language, Umbundu, is a Western Bantu language of the Niger-Congo family.

TIMELINE

1500s	Ovimbundu emerge in the Benguela highlands.
1600	First contact and trade with the Portuguese.
c.1800	The first Ovimbundu kingdoms develop.
1830	Portugal officially abolishes the slave trade.
1872	Rise of the Ovimbundu–Portuguese rubber trade.
1902–03	Ovimbundu lead Bailundo War, an uprising against the Portuguese prompted by the declining rubber trade.
1911	Rubber trade collapses and many Ovimbundu starve.
1966	Formation of the Ovimbundu-dominated UNITA.
1975	Angola wins independence; war breaks out between UNITA and Soviet-backed Angolan government.
1989	Cuban and South African troops leave Angola.
1994	Lusaka accord peace agreement is agreed.
1998	Fighting between UNITA and MPLA resumes after a ceasefire breakdown.
2002	Jonas Savimbi is killed; UNITA transforms itself into a nonmilitary, political organization.

ANGOLA'S LARGEST ETHNIC GROUP ARE THE OVIMBUNDU. FORMERLY A MAJOR TRADING PEOPLE WHO BENEFITED FROM THE LATE 19TH-CENTURY RUBBER BOOM, MORE RECENTLY, THEY PLAYED A LEADING ROLE IN ANGOLA'S STRUGGLE FOR INDEPENDENCE.

HISTORY

The Ovimbundu arose in the 16th–17th centuries as Jaga invaders intermingled with the peoples of the Benguela highlands in central Angola. The Ovimbundu traded with the Portuguese from around 1600 onward, mainly in slaves. Successful trading entrepreneurs formed an elite class in Ovimbundu society called the *olofumbelo*.

In the late 19th century the slave trade was largely replaced by rubber, which the Ovimbundu tapped in the forests. Yet when the rubber boom collapsed at the beginning of the 20th century, famine and conflict ensued and the Ovimbundu lost their political and economic independence. Under Portuguese rule they were forced to farm cash crops.

In the independence struggle in Angola in the late 1960s the Ovimbundu were prominent in the UNITA (União Nacional para a Independência Total de Angola) guerrilla movement. After independence in 1975, UNITA continued to fight the Angolan government. In 1994 UNITA reached a peace agreement with the Angolan government, but fighting erupted again. The death of its founder Jonas Savimbi in 2002 brought the long conflict to an uneasy close.

SOCIETY AND DAILY LIFE

The Ovimbundu grow a variety of cash crops, of which corn is the most important. Beans, manioc, potatoes, and coffee are also grown. Farming is mainly carried out by women and children, while men are

An Ovimbundu woman processing fish on a quayside. Many Ovimbundu have migrated to cities and now lead an urban way of life.

Precolonial Ovimbundu society was male dominated, with the men of a village exercising power as a group. Matrilineal inheritance (through the female line) was recognized where wealth and property were concerned, but political power came through membership of a male kinship group. The male members of such groups were called *oluse* (also the name given to the house where they met). Today these groups have declined in significance and the nuclear family is now the main social unit.

CULTURE AND RELIGION

The Ovimbundu religion assigns great importance to respect for the ancestors and to divination. The spirits of the ancestors are offered gifts to ensure that they favor their living relatives. Diviners known as *ochimbanda* are responsible for finding out the causes of sickness, death, and other ills, which are thought to be the result of witchcraft. They do this by using a "divining basket" containing important ritual objects. Roman Catholic and Protestant missionaries converted many Ovimbundu in the colonial era. Many Ovimbundu combine Christian values and beliefs with preexisting practices.

SEE ALSO: *Christianity; Festival and ceremony; Music and musical instruments; Sculpture.*

responsible for hunting. Livestock is also kept, including sheep, goats, and cattle. Some Ovimbundu people still sell forest products such as beeswax.

Under colonialism large numbers of Ovimbundu men migrated to work on plantations and in factories, and now live in the more impoverished districts of Angolan cities. Although this development disrupted traditional society, most Ovimbundu still live in a rural environment.

THE OVIMBUNDU AND UNITA

The guerrilla group UNITA (standing for, in Portuguese, "The Union for the Complete Independence of Angola") was formed in 1966 by the Ovimbundu Jonas Savimbi. During the independence struggle against Portugal, this group came into conflict with the Soviet- and Cuban-backed Marxist MPLA movement. UNITA embraced pro-Western policies and drew support from the United States and apartheid South Africa. Mainly funded by diamond and ivory smuggling, UNITA ran a parallel state, including educational and health services, in the Ovimbundu heartland. But the long civil war brought great hardship to the ordinary Ovimbundu. The destruction of roads and other services that occurred still affects most of Angola's rural population. As a political party UNITA remains opposed to the MPLA regime.

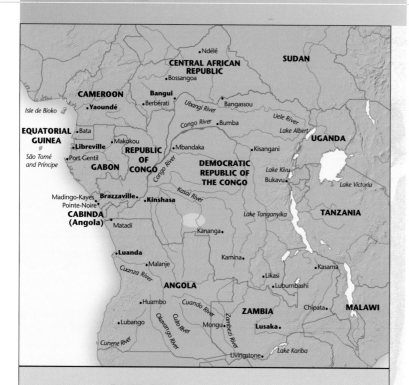

FACT FILE

Population	c.250,000, all in the DRC
Religion	Christianity; preexisting beliefs
Language	The Pende language, Kipende, is a Central Bantu tongue of the wider Niger-Congo language family.

TIMELINE

c.1620   Pende migrate north from Angola into their present territory in the Democratic Republic of Congo (DRC).

c.1685   The Pende settle at Mashita Mbanza (present-day DRC).

1885   Chokwe expand north into Pende territory. The Berlin Conference establishes the Congo Free State.

1903–13   Pende exploited as forced labor in rubber plantations.

1931   Pende stage a failed uprising against the Belgians.

1932   The Pende are divided along the Loange River into two different administrative areas, Kasai and Bandundu.

1960   Congo (Kinshasa) wins independence from Belgium.

1963–65   Pende and Mbuun rebel against Congolese regime.

1965   Mobutu Sese Seko seizes power in a coup in Congo.

1971   Congo (Kinshasa) renamed Zaïre.

1997–2001   Mobutu is ousted by Laurent Kabila. A long period of civil war ensues until Kabila is assassinated.

2002–03   Foreign forces leave the Democratic Republic of the Congo (formerly Zaire) as interim government is set up.

T HE PENDE LIVE ON THE SAVANNA AND BUSHLANDS OF THE SOUTHERN AND CENTRAL DEMOCRATIC REPUBLIC OF THE CONGO. THE EASTERN AND WESTERN PENDE EACH HAVE THEIR OWN CULTURAL TRADITIONS.

HISTORY

According to their own oral histories, the Pende originally came from Angola, but migrated north in the 17th century to escape the Portuguese slave trade. They eventually settled in their present territory and then expanded eastward, some reaching as far as the Kasai River. In the 18th century they were under the control of the Lunda state. Late in the 19th century the Pende were invaded by the Chokwe, forcing many to flee farther north, where they resisted the Chokwe until the whole region came under European control. The Congo Free State was established as a private colony of the Belgian King Leopold II in 1885 and the Pende were forced to work in appalling conditions on rubber and palm-oil plantations.

An attempt by the Pende living west of the Kwilu River to rebel against colonial rule in 1932 was brutally suppressed by the authorities. After independence in 1960, the Pende and neighboring groups rose up against the new government of Congo (Kinshasa). The period of violence following the rebellion caused the deaths of many thousands of Pende, particularly older people. Homes and fields were abandoned and many longstanding customs were given up during these difficult times.

DAILY LIFE AND SOCIETY

The Pende live mainly as a farming people, growing corn, millet, cassava, and plantains as their staple crops. Agricultural work, domestic chores, and raising children are generally carried out by women, while the tasks of hunting and fishing are usually performed by men. Men also help with heavier types of agricultural work, such as clearing the fields. Surplus food and supplies are sold in local markets by women. Among the Pende it is not considered appropriate for men to sit with women and children while eating, and so they eat separately.

The Pende have a strong sense of their shared history (the migration from Angola) and common ancestry. The term *Pende* is used by the people themselves and is not a name that has been given to them by outsiders. Pende society is fairly equal; although there are chiefs, they play a largely symbolic role and have little power. The Pende are matrilineal, meaning that inheritance and relations are traced through the female line. The main authority figure for a Pende man is therefore his mother's brother, rather than his own father. Age-sets (*indongo*) are another important feature of Pende society, with all men of a particular initiation generation grouping together.

RELIGION AND CULTURE

The religious beliefs of the Pende include reverence for ancestors (*mvumbi*), who are prayed to and given offerings in order to bring about success in everyday life and challenges. The ancestors are thought to accompany their descendants in the world of the living, and to make their voices heard in the wind rustling through the grass. The Pende also believe in a supreme creator god, Maweze, who made the earth and everything in it. Sorcery, which the Pende call *wanga*, is regarded as the ability to influence the world for personal gain. Unlike in many other African witchcraft traditions, *wanga* is not necessarily negative. However, the Pende disapprove of people who display too much talent and success in their lives, who are accused of overusing *wanga*. Christianity, which was introduced to the region during the colonial period, is having an increasing impact on the Pende.

SEE ALSO: Chokwe; Christianity; Festival and ceremony; Lunda; Masks and masquerade.

PENDE INITIATION RITES AND MASQUERADES

The Pende perform masquerades on many ritual occasions. These include boys' initiation ceremonies, for which there are special masks collectively known as *minganji*. Across their territory the Pende use a wide variety of specific masks, such as *gitenga*, made from raffia fibers that have been dyed red and formed into a disk shape symbolizing the sun. Other male initiation masks take the form of dangerous local animals, including leopards, lions, snakes, elephants, and Cape buffaloes. These are not generally used in any other masquerades, large and powerful animals being particularly associated with masculinity. The Pende deliberately revived the customs of masks and masquerading in the 1950s, as a way of maintaining their own culture and traditions in the face of colonial rule.

Pende animal maskers perform a leopard dance at an initiation rite.

MAJOR WORKS AND THEIR AUTHORS

Title	Date	Author
O Segredo da Morta (The Dead Woman's Secret)	1934	António Assis Júnior
Sagrada Esperança (Sacred Hope)	1974	Agostinho Neto
Luuanda *A Cidade e a Infância* (City of Infants)	1975 1978	José Luandino Vieira
Sim Camarada (Yes Comrade) *Quem Me Dera Ser Onda* (If Only I were a Wave on the Sea) *Crónica de Um Mujimbo* (Chronicle of a Rumor)	1977 1982 1989	Manuel Rui Monteiro
"Mestre" Tamoda e Outros Contos ("Master" Tamoda and Other Stories) *O Ministro* (The Minister)	1977 1990	Xuantega Xitu
Mayombe *A Gloriosa Família* (The Glorious Family) *Jaime Bunda e a Morte do Americano* (Jaime Bunda and the Death of the American)	1980 1997 2003	Pepetela
Poemas (Poems)	1982	António Jacinto
Naçao Crioula (Creole Nation) *O Vendedor de Passados* (The Man Who Sold Pasts)	1997 2004	José Eduardo Agualusa
Quantas Madrugadas Tem a Noite (How Many Dawns has the Night)	2004	Ondjaki

ALL PORTUGUESE-LANGUAGE LITERATURE IN CENTRAL AFRICA COMES FROM ANGOLA. PORTUGAL ESTABLISHED A COLONY THERE IN THE LATE 1500s, AND ONLY QUIT THE COUNTRY IN 1975. PORTUGUESE REMAINS THE OFFICIAL LANGUAGE AND ITS MAIN MEDIUM FOR LITERARY EXPRESSION.

HISTORICAL DEVELOPMENT

Portuguese literature was the first body of writing in a modern European language to emerge in Africa. As early as 1540, the ruler of the kingdom of Kongo, Afonso I (d.1545), was sending elegantly written letters to the Portuguese asking for their protection from frequent slave raids on his country. Later, most of the early literature from the Portuguese colony of Angola was dominated by white intellectuals, many of whom were interested in collecting and recording African oral traditions and folklore.

With some notable exceptions, the literature of Angola from the 20th century until the present day has been dominated by

An Angolan practicing his reading skills in Portuguese with a grammar book in that language. Despite the bitter legacy of centuries of rule by Portugal, Angola has kept Portuguese as its official language to avoid favoring one native language group.

mestico writers (*mestico* is the Portuguese term for a person of mixed European and African descent). Historically, the *mestico* class formed the political, social, and economic elite in Angolan society. This group arose from intermarriage between the Portuguese and prominent black Africans who were important middlemen in the transatlantic slave trade from the 16th to the 19th century. In literary terms, the legacy of this is that it is often difficult in Angolan literature to tell a person's racial background from their writing. Unusually among postindependence African countries, the white, black, and *mestico* authors are all concerned with the same issues.

INDEPENDENCE AND BEYOND

The most important figures in Angolan literature were the intellectuals and activists who took part in the independence struggle of the 1960s and early 1970s. They include Agostinho Neto (Angola's first president after 1975), António Jacinto (b.1924), José Luandino Vieira (b.1935), Xuantega Xitu (b.1924), and Pepetela (b.1941). The main theme of these writers was the oppressive nature of the colonial regime and its systematic abuses of civil rights. They set this in contrast with the pride and dignity of the Angolan people. Many of these writers were imprisoned by the Portuguese during the 1960s on the Cape Verde Islands. Since most of this generation's best works were written while they were in jail, they remained unknown until the late 1970s.

Many writers who made their name during the liberation struggle have continued to produce poetry and novels. Pepetela, for example, who served in the Angolan government in the early years of independence, has published works strongly criticizing the failures of the postcolonial Angolan state.

Younger authors, in addition to writing about the legacy of the independence struggle, have also diversified to cover a

AGOSTINHO NETO

Dr. António Agostinho Neto (1922–79) was one of the key literary and historical figures of modern Angola. Born as the son of a Protestant pastor in a small village near the capital, Luanda, he began studying medicine in Portugal in 1947. He was one of the most prominent intellectuals in the movement for Angolan independence and was imprisoned by the Portuguese authorities in 1951. In 1962 Neto returned to Angola and joined the organized resistance to colonial rule. He was elected leader of the Movimento Popular de Libertaçao de Angola (MPLA; Popular Movement for the Liberation of Angola) that year and became Angola's first president after independence in 1975. His writings were part of his efforts to end colonial domination, and his poetry won much international acclaim, particularly his collection *Sagrada Esperança* (Sacred Hope; 1974), in which he described the urgent need for independence and the hardships (forced labor, beatings, starvation) suffered by the victims of colonialism.

wider range of issues, such as racial identity. For example the novel *O Vendedor de Passados* (2004) by José Agualusa tells the story of a man called Félix Ventura, who falsifies documents for rich clients in modern Luanda in order to help them "prove" their (mixed-race European and African) ancestry.

Agostinho Neto addressing a meeting. His dreams of an independent Angola were realized in 1975, but the country was immediately plunged into more than 25 years of civil war.

SEE ALSO: *African-language literature; French-language literature; Kongo; Oral literature; Ovimbundu.*

SCULPTURE

CENTRAL AFRICA IS FAMED FOR ITS SOPHISTICATED SCULPTURES. IN THIS HEAVILY FORESTED REGION, WOOD IS THE MOST COMMON MATERIAL. HOWEVER COPPER, IRON, IVORY, POTTERY, AND EVEN STONE HAVE ALSO BEEN USED BY SCULPTORS.

European and U.S. scholars and artists have long been captivated by the sculptures of Central Africa. Accordingly, these sculptures are extensively studied by experts, highly prized by collectors, and given a prominent place in museum collections. Yet the people who created these diverse sculptures did not think of them as works of art but as objects that had specific social purposes.

SCULPTURE AND SOCIETY

In Central African cultures, sculptures are often associated with magical or spiritual properties. They may act as vessels for the spirits of ancestors and important individuals. The royal portrait figures (*ndop*) of the Kuba, for example, were thought of as "soul doubles" of the king they depicted, and the safety of the sculpture and well-being of the king were believed to be related. After the death of the king the figure was kept as a memorial and was often regarded as actually containing the king's spirit. These figures were displayed publicly on major ceremonial occasions and regularly polished with palm or camwood oil to give them a rich, reddish sheen. Other royal sculptures were prestige objects and acted as symbols of royal authority. Sculptures of this type include the elaborate stools and chairs of the Lunda and Chokwe and the wooden staffs that were carried by Ovimbundu men as status symbols. The ends of these staffs were carved into the shape of human figures,

Objects sometimes misleadingly called "fetishes" are also an important part of the sculptural tradition of Central Africa. The *minkinsi* figures of the Kongo were used for various purposes, including healing, bringing about good fortune, divination, and protecting people from witchcraft. *Nkisi nkondi* were figures in the form of hunters and were stabbed with iron blades or nails during divination ceremonies. This ritual act was supposed to cause similar injuries to witches. The "power figures" of the Yaka and Suku fulfilled a similar role. These had no potency in themselves but contained hollows holding spiritually charged substances called *bilongo* or *bashimba,* such as clay, seeds, leaves, cowrie shells, mirrors, or parts of animals.

Reliquary figures are used to protect the remains of ancestors. The *tumba* figures of the Kongo and *bieri* figures of the Fang sat on top of vessels containing the bones of the

A sculptor carving a piece of ivory. Ivory was once a favorite material for making prestigious objects and tourist goods. Its use is now restricted by conservation measures to protect elephant herds.

Phemba figures such as this were used by the female Mpemba society of the Kongo, which was founded by a midwife to promote fertility.

dead and were used in rituals to contact the ancestors. Many of these exquisite Fang figures were destroyed by Christian missionaries, who mistook them for idols. Yet it was precisely because such figures were not sacred to the Fang (being far less important than the bones they guarded) that they were willing to sell them to Europeans.

An interesting early 20th-century sculptor was the Woyo potter Voania Muba. His terracotta groups of figures and riders on horseback have African features, but were also influenced by English Staffordshire pottery imported to the Congo during the colonial period. Muba also signed his work, so marking a shift from the African sculptural tradition to conscious "art" produced largely for the European market.

SEE ALSO: Contemporary art; Fang; Festival and ceremony; Kongo; Kuba; Lunda; Masks and masquerade.

LEANDRO MBOMIO NSUE

The Central African sculptor Leandro Mbomio Nsue is known for using metal in his works. He was born in Equatorial Guinea in 1938 and studied in Spain during the 1960s. His father and grandfather were Fang carvers who made wooden masks and *bieri* figures. His masklike sculpture *Mascara Bifronte*, cast in bronze, blends elements of traditional Fang wooden sculpture with Western art influences. Interestingly, many leading artists in the West in the 20th century were influenced by African sculpture, including Pablo Picasso, who was inspired by the abstract features of Fang masks when developing his Cubist style. Nsue's work has certain affinities with Cubism, but he approaches his work first and foremost from an African rather than a Western perspective.

MAJOR BROADCASTING ORGANIZATIONS

Country	Broadcasters	Ownership
Angola	Televisião Popular de Angola	State
	Radio Nacional de Angola	State
	Radio Ecclesia	Roman Catholic
	Luanda-Antena comercial	Private
Central African Republic	Télévision Centrafricaine	State
	Radio Centrafrique	State
	Radio Notre Dame	Roman Catholic
	Radio Nostalgie	Private
	Radio Ndeke Luka	United Nations
Cameroon	Cameroon Radio-Télévision	State
	TV Max	Private
	Radio Reine	Roman Catholic
	Radio Siantou	Private
Equatorial Guinea	Television Nacional	State
	Radio Nacional de Guinea Ecuatorial	State
	Radio Asonga	Private (president's son)
Republic of Congo	TV Congo	State
	Radio Congo	State
	Radio Brazzaville	State
	Radio Liberté	Private
DRC	Radio-Télévision Nationale Congolaise	State
	Canal Z	Private
	Attenne A	Private
	La Voix du Congo	State
	Radio Okapi	United Nations
	Raga FM	Private
Zambia	Zambia National Broadcasting Corporation	State
	Radio Phoenix	Private
	Yatsani Radio	Roman Catholic
	Radio Choice	Private

In the town of Bunia, in the Democratic Republic of the Congo, a young boy tunes a radio with a makeshift sound system. Many people in the DRC kept in touch with current events via radio during the violence that swept the country in 1997–2003.

COLONIALISM INTRODUCED TELEVISION AND RADIO TO CENTRAL AFRICA. WHILE TELEVISION IS STILL LARGELY CONFINED TO WEALTHY URBAN POPULATIONS, RADIO IS MORE WIDELY AVAILABLE, REACHING MANY PEOPLE IN RURAL AREAS. THE ADVENT OF MASS MEDIA HAS HAD MAJOR POLITICAL AND CULTURAL IMPLICATIONS FOR CENTRAL AFRICAN SOCIETIES.

MASS MEDIA AND GOVERNMENT

In almost all Central African countries, freedom of speech in the media is restricted. State-owned television and radio stations tend to be most widely received by the general public, and these broadcasters usually reflect the views of the administration. In particular, Central African leaders have often used television as a means of creating an idealized image of themselves and increasing their popularity. The degree of media freedom varies from state to state. In the Democratic Republic of the Congo (DRC) it is dangerous to criticize the government or to attempt to expose political corruption, whereas in the neighboring Republic of Congo, there is much greater freedom. Some attempts have been made by a few Central African governments to liberalize the media and introduce competition but these have not been entirely successful. For example, the lifting of restrictions on private radio and television stations in Cameroon in 2000 was followed by a return to more repressive

Today, practices such as the talking drum have almost been wiped out by radio and television. Modern communications technologies have brought about a major shift in the way information is spread in Central Africa. Initiation ceremonies, in which young people were taught about the rights, responsibilities and rituals of adulthood, are no longer the only ways to receive knowledge. The information that is available to any given individual no longer depends on gender, seniority, and status. Accordingly, the importance of older methods of communication has declined. Television and radio signals are broadcast from central locations, often in major cities, and this has meant that the ability of rural populations to control the knowledge available in their societies has diminished. The social changes that have come about through mass communication technologies are, as would be expected, more obvious in urban areas where ownership of receiving devices and signal reception are greatest.

Angolan children watching a TV show. Television ownership in Central Africa is still mainly confined to towns.

SEE ALSO: Christianity; English-language literature; Marriage and the family; Movies.

policies after 2003. The mass media can also be used as a platform to attack the ruling regime as well as to support it, such as with Radio de l'Alliance, an illegal antigovernment station formed in 1993 in the DRC (then Zaïre) to oppose the dictatorship of Mobutu Sese Seko.

SOCIAL IMPACT OF MASS MEDIA

Increased ownership and use of radios and televisions over the past few decades has had a major social and cultural impact on Central African societies. Before mass communication technologies came to this region, ideas and information could not be transmitted instantaneously across vast areas. Formal communication between and within villages was usually conducted by means of the talking drum. Secret messages were encoded in drumbeats, and this cipher was known only to a group of senior men. Drumming was an elite activity and controlling this mode of communication was one of the ways in which such individuals maintained their high social status.

RADIO AND PUBLIC HEALTH EDUCATION

Thanks to the limited access that most people in Central Africa have to formal education (particularly in rural areas) governments in the region often make use of mass media to put across vital information relating to public health. For example, in 1991–92, the Zambian Health Education Unit broadcast a radio program called *Nshilakamona*, a soap opera about two families living in the capital Lusaka and their attempts to deal with HIV/AIDS. It was broadcast in Bemba, the most widely spoken language in Zambia after English. Audience research was carried out throughout the period when this drama was shown. Its findings were that people were more aware of how to prevent HIV/AIDS after the screenings than they had been before. Such initiatives are limited by the fact that, in rural areas, many people still do not have a radio of their own. On the other hand, it is estimated that two-thirds of Zambians have access to radio broadcasts, even if they have to visit friends and family to hear them. This makes radio the most widely available form of mass media in the country.

TODAY MOST FABRICS USED AND WORN IN CENTRAL AFRICA ARE IMPORTED FROM THE FAR EAST OR EUROPE. HOWEVER, BEFORE THE COLONIAL ERA THE REGION'S MAIN TEXTILES WERE RAFFIA AND BARK CLOTH. PORTUGUESE TRADERS TOOK HOME RAFFIA SAMPLES AS EXAMPLES OF AFRICAN CRAFTS. TRADITIONAL TEXTILES NOW PLAY A LARGELY CEREMONIAL ROLE.

RAFFIA AND BARK CLOTH

Raffia cloth is produced from the young leaves of the raffia palm. Lengths of about 6 inches (15 cm) are cut from the upper part of the raffia leaves, and then left to dry in the sun. After drying the lengths are split into thinner strands, either with a comb or by hand, and the resulting fibers are then ready for weaving. Raffia cloth is generally made within the Congo Basin area.

Bark cloth is made from tree bark, which is removed from the trunk in strips and moistened. The moist bark is then beaten with a hammer to expand it, often more

(Below) Women sell printed cotton cloth at a market in the Zambian capital Lusaka. Cotton has long been produced in Central Africa. Modern machine-spinning has replaced hand-spun manufacture, but cheap imports are threatening the industry.

(Right) The Kuba of the Democratic Republic of the Congo are renowned for making fine textiles. Their craftspeople are highly skilled at weaving intricate geometric designs into raffia cloth. Here, a Kuba man sits at a loom weaving a mat.

than four times its original area. Sections of bark cloth are then sewn together. Bark cloth is felted rather than woven. It is produced in the Congo Basin and in Malawi.

THE SOCIAL ROLE OF TEXTILES

Textiles have always been regarded as valuable and prestigious items in Central Africa, thanks to the slow, labor-intensive and painstaking processes involved in their manufacture. Raffia cloth, for example, was widely used as a currency by Central African societies in the colonial and precolonial eras. Made in pieces roughly 14 inches (35 cm) square, called *mbongo* (singular *libongo*), the cloth was bundled together in units of 4, 10, 20, 40, or 100 and used as money. The Portuguese even tried to stamp the *mbongo* with their royal coat of arms as if they were metal coins.

Raffia and bark cloth are used for a wide variety of ceremonial occasions: to display newborn babies, at initiations, as bridewealth, at funerals, and as payment of court fines or in legal settlements. Men are responsible for growing the plants, harvesting them, and weaving the cloth, while women usually decorate the finished items. However, there are some notable exceptions to this general rule. Kuba men, for instance, decorate their own skirts and

are renowned for their wide repertoire of skills, which includes embroidery, appliqué, patchwork, and dyeing. Cloth decoration by the Kuba duplicates the patterns that are found on their wood carvings. Bark cloth is considered to be the clothing of the ancestors in many Central African cultures, and raffia cloth is still widely thought of as the only suitable material for burial.

Textiles did not attract the interest of artists and collectors in the West as immediately as, say, sculpture. Yet when they did come to public attention, some major 20th-century European artists such as Paul Klee and Henri Matisse were inspired by the abstract designs of Central African cloth.

SEE ALSO: Contemporary art; Festival and ceremony; Kuba; Mbuti, Twa, and Mbenga; Music and musical instruments.

MBUTI BARK CLOTH DECORATION

The Mbuti people of the Ituri Forest in the Democratic Republic of the Congo are well known for the pieces of patterned bark cloth (*pongo*) they produce. Mbuti men felt the cloth; women are responsible for decorating it by coloring it with gardenia juice and black carbon. The designs are highly abstract, consisting of lines of varying lengths and directions, and are regarded as sacred by the Mbuti. The patterns are not random decoration but relate to the sound patterns of the polyphonic yodeling for which the Mbuti are also famous. The various lines and motifs criss-cross each other and wander across the surface of the cloth, producing stark contrasts in the decoration of the fabric from one section to the next.

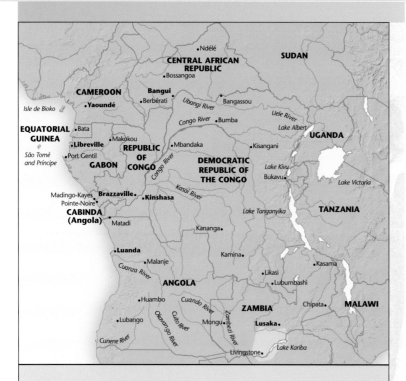

FACT FILE

Population	c.1,000,000 Tonga in Zambia; 140,000 in Zimbabwe
Religion	Preexisting beliefs; Christianity
Language	The Tonga language, Chitonga, and several related dialects, belong to the Central Bantu branch of the Niger-Congo language family.

TIMELINE

1830	Emergence of the Lozi and Ndebele kingdoms, both of which make frequent slave raids on the Tonga.
1889	British South Africa Company annexes the Tonga area.
1902	Tonga stage unsuccessful rebellion against British rule.
1905	First schools and missions are built in the Tonga area.
1953	Northern Rhodesia (modern Zambia), Southern Rhodesia (modern Zimbabwe), and Nyasaland (modern Malawi) form the Central African Federation (CAF).
1964	Northern Rhodesia wins independence and is renamed Zambia. The Central African Federation disintegrates.
1965	White-minority-ruled Southern Rhodesia declares its independence from Britain. The Tonga are divided by the Zambia–Rhodesia border.
1979–80	The white regime in Rhodesia falls; the country is renamed Zimbabwe and becomes independent.
1991	First multiparty elections held in Zambia.
2005	Droughts cause major food shortages in Zambia.

HISTORY

A Bantu-speaking people, the Tonga are thought to have migrated to their current territory at some stage over the last 1,000 years. For most of the 19th century the Tonga were sandwiched between two major powers, the Lozi and Ndebele kingdoms. First contact with Europeans came in the 1853, when the Scottish missionary and explorer David Livingstone (1813–73) visited the region. In 1889 the British South Africa Company of the colonialist Cecil Rhodes gained control of the area that covered the Tonga territory.

Under colonialism, the Tonga were often relocated and put in reservations. The largest such resettlement came when the Kariba Dam on the Zambezi River reached completion in 1958. Since the mid-1960s the Tonga have been divided by the Zimbabwe–Zambia border. Economic differences have subsequently developed; because the Zambian Tonga enjoy better communications with neighboring areas, they have had less need to become migrant laborers to provide an income than the Tonga of Zimbabwe.

SOCIETY AND DAILY LIFE

The Tonga are an agricultural people who mostly grow corn, sorghum, and bulrush millet. Those who live in the more fertile Zambezi Valley plant their crops in the same place each year and plots of land are owned and inherited by groups of related

individuals. In contrast, the Plateau Tonga move from place to place as the soil becomes exhausted. Cattle are kept in large numbers by the Plateau Tonga, but are much less common among the Gwembe Tonga. Men and young boys clear the land, plow the fields with oxen, and herd cattle. Women and young girls plant seeds and harvest the crop, in addition to preparing food and brewing beer. Since the 1930s cash crops have been widely grown for export, particularly in Zambia.

In the past, Tonga society did not have any hierarchy (a rigid social class order), and people enjoyed mostly equal status. Unlike their neighbors, the Tonga have never been organized into a kingdom or other centralized state. Tonga society is matrilineal—people trace their ancestry and inherit property and rights through their mother's line of descent.

CULTURE AND RELIGION

Tonga religion focuses on the belief in ancestor spirits (*mizimu*). These spirits are given sacrificial offerings on special occasions, such as when moving house or planting crops. When a misfortune occurs, a diviner is consulted, who will discover whether a particular ancestral spirit has been offended and requires a special sacrifice to be made. The Tonga also believe in a creator god called Leza, who has no direct involvement in most human affairs. Other types of spirits are also revered, including those called the *basangu* (see box feature), and the *zelo*, which are evil ghosts. Belief in many of these spirits has declined as a result of the rise of Christianity among the Tonga. There has also been a blending of preexisting religious practices and Christian ideas.

See also: Festival and ceremony; Lozi; Music and musical instruments.

Tonga women with babies strapped on their backs prepare to fish on Lake Kariba. The building of the dam that formed this lake flooded large parts of the Zambezi River valley and forced many Gwembe Tonga to move.

TONGA RAIN SHRINES

Rain shrines (*malende*) are still an important focus for Tonga rituals, although they are not so widely used as in the past. The shrine may be a natural object, such as hollow fig tree, or a small hut made by people. The shrines are associated with the *basangu* spirits, which act as intermediaries between people and the creator god. The Tonga sing and dance to persuade the *basangu* to bring rain, and sacrifice and eat a chicken. The next day beer is brought to the shrines, where it is drunk and also poured over the doorway as an offering to the spirits. Rain shrines generally serve a small group of villages, and before colonialism the rain shrine ceremony was one of the few events that regularly linked and brought together all the Tonga of a particular area.

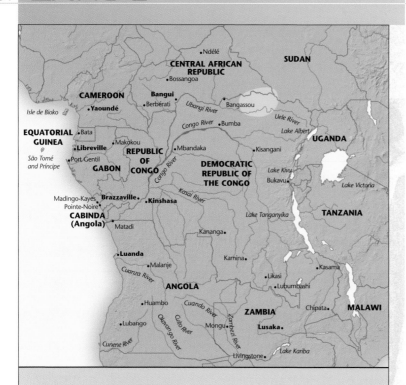

FACT FILE

Population	3,800,000 mostly in the DRC; smaller populations in Sudan and the Central African Republic
Religion	Christianity; preexisting religious practices
Language	Several dialects of Zande are spoken, all of which are mutually intelligible and are part of the Adamawa-Ubangi branch of the Niger-Congo language family.

TIMELINE

c.1 c.e.	Adamawa-Ubangi speaking peoples establish themselves in the northern part of Central Africa.
c.1750	Zande principalities emerge under rule of Avongara clan.
c.1800	Zande begin their eastward expansion north of the Uele River and into the Bomu Valley.
1841	Mehmet Ali's Sudan expedition enters Zandeland.
1868–69	Zanzibari slave raiding parties arrive in Zandeland.
1880	Zande area annexed by Egyptian province of Equatoria.
1891	Belgian Congo Free State seizes southern Zande area
1960	The Central African Republic and Congo (present-day Democratic Republic of the Congo) win independence.
1965	Mobutu Sese Seko seizes power in a coup in Congo.
1996	Mobutu is ousted in a coup by Laurent Kabila. A long period of civil war ensues until Kabila is assassinated.
2002–03	Foreign forces withdraw from the Democratic Republic of the Congo and an interim government is established.

THE ZANDE (OR AZANDE) MAINLY INHABIT THE DEMOCRATIC REPUBLIC OF THE CONGO AND SOUTHERN SUDAN, WITH SMALLER NUMBERS ALSO LIVING IN THE CENTRAL AFRICAN REPUBLIC.

HISTORY

Like the more widespread and numerous Bantu-speaking peoples of Africa, the Zande also descend from peoples who migrated from West Africa into Central Africa from around 1000 B.C.E. to 1000 C.E. Unlike the Bantu peoples, the speakers of Adamawa-Ubangi languages, including the Zande, remained confined to northeastern areas of Central Africa.

The first Zande states emerged in the 18th century, with the rise of the Ambomu people led by the ruling Avongara clan, who successfully overran nearby peoples. By the 1800s they had begun to expand the territory under their control eastward. The name *Zande* literally means "those who possess much land," in reference to this time of conquests. The first contact between the Zande and foreign peoples came in 1841, when an expedition sent by the Egyptian ruler Mehmet Ali to conquer the Sudan arrived in this region. By the 1860s the area had begun to attract slave raiders from the Sultanate of Zanzibar. The Congolese portion of Zande territory was incorporated into the Belgian King Leopold II's Congo Free State in 1891 and power was taken away from local rulers over the following decades. The Sudanese part was absorbed into the Anglo-Egyptian Condominium in 1899; there, efforts were also made to break the power of the ruling Avongara princes.

In the 1920s the Sudanese colonial government changed its approach and decided to reinforce the status of the Avongara clan by incorporating it into the state structure while granting it some self-rule. The colonial administration also tried to raise the Zande's living standards by resettling them and (unsuccessfully) setting them up as large-scale cotton producers.

SOCIETY AND DAILY LIFE

The Zande are settled farmers, whose staple crop is millet. They also grow corn, cassava, sweet potatoes, peanuts, and bananas, using shifting cultivation and field rotation systems of farming. Tobacco and cotton are also grown as cash crops. The presence in this region of the tsetse fly, which carries the deadly disease trypanosomasis (sleeping sickness), prevents the Zande from keeping cattle or other livestock. Chickens are kept, although their main use was formerly in

divination rituals (see box feature) rather than as a food source. To supplement their diet, wild seeds and fungi are gathered, and hunting is conducted with dogs.

Zande society is based on a rigid social order of classes (a hierarchy). Supreme power once lay in the hands of the princes of the ruling Avongara clan, who created the

ZANDE ORACLES

The Zande practice divination by consulting oracles. Oracles are ritual means by which people can investigate the source and causes of witchcraft in their lives. In the past, they were often used in village court cases to decide on an individual's guilt or innocence. The cheapest and least sophisticated type of oracle is the *iwa*, or friction oracle. This involves a piece of wood being dipped in a gourd full of water and rubbed against a carved board, while the diviner asks questions. Whether the response is negative or affirmative will depend on whether or not the rubbing implement sticks or moves with ease. The termite oracle, called *dakpa*, is considered to be more reliable and involves offering branches from two different species of tree to termites. Which type the termites choose determines the response to the question. *Benge*, the poison oracle, is the most expensive and thought to be the most trustworthy. A solution based on strychnine, a deadly poison, is rubbed on the beak of a chicken, and if the chicken dies the response is affirmative (or, if it is being used in trials, proves the guilt of the accused). *Benge* is only used for the most serious of issues, such as death, adultery, or illness.

A Zande diviner with a feathered headdress. People consult diviners to find out when the best time might be for, say, planting crops.

precolonial Zande states. The princes held courts that passed judgement on disputes and crimes, including allegations of witchcraft. The oracle of a prince was the highest authority in Zande divination practices and could never be wrong. Colonialism greatly reduced the authority of the princes.

The Zande practice polygyny (the custom of a man marrying more than one woman), although the need to pay bridewealth (usually with spears) makes it more common among wealthier men. In the past the Avongara nobility often took so many wives that there was a shortage of women available for ordinary men to marry.

ARTS AND CRAFTS

Zande craftspeople are famous for their metalworking and woodcarving skills. Among the objects produced in the past by Zande blacksmiths was the *shongo*, a multibladed throwing knife. This fearsome weapon measured up to 2.5 feet (76 cm) in length and was generally aimed at the legs of enemies. It was ingeniously designed and weighted to spin in flight and so inflict maximum damage. Another type of Azande knife was shaped like a sickle. Blacksmiths often intricately engraved or embossed one side of the blades they manufactured.

YANDA FIGURES

The Zande were renowned for producing small sculptures made of wood or fired clay. These statuettes, which generally depict ancestors or animal figures, are around 3–10 inches (8–25 cm) high and have very simplified features and enlarged heads. One particular type of female figurine, called the *yanda*, was associated with a secret society known as the Mani and was named for the guardian spirit of that society. The Mani society represented the interests of Zande people who were traditionally excluded from power, such as women, but its ideals put it at odds with the ruling Zande princes. The chief of the Mani society would infuse the *yanda* figure with his magical powers by blowing smoke on it and rubbing a china-clay paste into it. The *yanda* statuettes were thought to protect society members from illness, hunting accidents, and evil spirits, and were used in divination ceremonies.

Zande wood carvings included the *yanda* figures used for divination and a wide variety of musical instruments. Slit drums, wooden bells, xylophonelike instruments known as *sanza*, and bow-harps were made in the form of human or animal figures (see MUSIC AND MUSICAL INSTRUMENTS).

CULTURE AND RELIGION

The Zande have a strong belief in witchcraft. In particular, they believe that sons inherit witchcraft powers from their fathers.

Misfortune or illnesses are often attributed to the influence of a witch, and if a Zande person has an accident or falls sick, he or she will consult an oracle with the help of a ritual specialist to discover the culprit (see box feature, p.105).

The fact that so much is known about the divination rituals of the Zande is due to the work of a British anthropologist, Edward Evans-Pritchard (1902–73). In the 1930s, Evans-Pritchard spent a long time studying their cultural and religious practices.

The Zande believe in a creator god, Mboli, and respect for ancestors is still strong; the Avongara once maintained a royal ancestor cult. Although Christianity, especially Roman Catholicism, has become widespread, it has been blended with and modified by preexisting religious practices. For the Zande the threat of witchcraft is ever-present and Christianity provides little defense against it.

Zande children in a classroom in the north of the Democratic Republic of the Congo. Like other Congolese peoples, the lives of the Zande were seriously disrupted by the civil war that raged from 1997 to 2002.

SEE ALSO: *Festival and ceremony; Mbuti, Twa, and Mbenga; Metalwork; Sculpture.*

Any of the words printed in SMALL CAPITAL LETTERS can be looked up in this glossary.

adobe Dried clay or mud, widely used as a building material throughout Africa.

age-grades The different social level in certain societies. Each person is part of an "age-set" (a group of similar-aged peers) who move up as they grow older through the various age-grades, gaining in status.

agriculturalist A settled (sedentary) farmer who makes his or her living by cultivating crops.

banco A building material used in sub-Saharan Africa. It is similar to ADOBE, but is made using sun-dried blocks of clay reinforced with grain chaff (the leftovers after the cereal has been extracted).

basangu In the belief system of the Tonga, spirits that act as intermediaries between people and the creator god. They are associated with particular regions or neighborhoods.

benge A form of oracle involving poison, used by the Zande in DIVINATION rituals.

Berlin Conference on Africa A meeting held in 1884–85 to reduce tension between the European colonial powers by agreeing spheres of influence in Central Africa. It recognized Belgian King Leopold II's claim on the CONGO FREE STATE, and granted all countries free access to the Congo and Niger rivers.

bieri Figures made of wood and attached to RELIQUARY caskets holding the remains of ancestors by the Fang. The term came to be more generally applied to the veneration of ancestors among this people.

bilongo Spiritually charged substances placed within "power figures" (such as the NKISI NKONDI of the Kongo) to give them magical power during DIVINATION ceremonies.

bokulala A Mongo village chief.

bridewealth A common practice among African peoples, in which a marriage is sealed by a gift given by the groom to the family of the bride. This gift is often in the form of cattle, but may also be other livestock or money.

bushmeat The general term for wild animals that are killed for human consumption. Wildlife has always been taken in sustainable quantities by HUNTER-GATHERERS; however, growth in demand and new transport links have created a wider market for bushmeat. In the Central African rainforest, several species are now under threat of extinction from this trade.

bwaantshy The official regalia worn by the Kuba king.

bwiti A political–religious sect that developed among the Fang people of Gabon in the early 20th century and is still strong. It combines Christian elements with the ancestral reverence of the Fang religion (BIERI).

Chisungu A Benga initiation rite for admitting girls into womanhood.

clan A social group made up of several extended families or LINEAGES. Clan members often trace their descent from a common ancestor.

Congo Free State Region of Central Africa taken by Leopold II, King of the Belgians, as a personal colony. He sponsored exploration of the Congo River by H. M. Stanley in 1879–84. In Leopold's colony, rubber was tapped using slave labor; atrocities became widespread and the Belgian government was forced to take it over in 1908, as the Belgian Congo. The country is now called the Democratic Republic of the Congo.

Copperbelt A mining area in Zambia that is rich in copper, the country's chief export. It lies 200 miles (320 km) north of the capital; the Tan-Zam railroad, completed in 1975, linked the Copperbelt to Dar-es-Salaam in Tanzania. It was built with Chinese communist help to reduce Zambia's dependency on the rail route through white-minority-controlled Rhodesia (Zimbabwe) to the port of Beira (Sofala) in Mozambique.

dakpa A form of oracle used by the Zande. It involves termites being offered two different types of leaves to eat.

divination A feature of many African religions, divination is practiced by ritual specialists, who use a variety of tools to find out the cause of misfortune, accidents, or illness.

DRC Abbreviation for the Democratic Republic of the Congo. The country took this name when it achieved independence from Belgium in 1961. From 1971 to 1997 it was known as Zaïre; in 1997 it reverted to its former name. The DRC is sometimes called Congo (Kinshasa) to distinguish it from the neighboring Republic of Congo, or Congo (Brazzaville).

hunter-gatherers People who depend on wild resources for their food. They live by hunting wild animals, fishing, and gathering plant foods and other materials.

infibulation The custom of female circumcision (also called female genital mutilation). It is practiced by some African peoples, and involves sewing up the vulva. It is harmful to a girl's health and is strongly discouraged by health authorities and aid workers. Some countries have outlawed the practice.

Kimbanguist Church A charismatic church founded by the prophet Simon Kimbangu (1889–1951) in the Belgian Congo in 1921. It is the largest independent church in Africa.

Ku Mélan The initiation rite for young men among the Fang.

Kuomboka An annual festival held by the Lozi, in which the king and his people migrate to higher ground to escape the flooding of the Zambezi River.

lineage An extended family group that shares a common ancestor. If the society traces its origins to a male ancestor and descent is traced from father to son, the lineage is termed patrilineal. If the ancestor is female and descent is traced from mother to daughter, the lineage is matrilineal.

litunga A Lozi king.

makossa A type of Central African dance music from Cameroon.

Mani A popular secret society among the Zande people. The term was also used as the title of the ruler of the Kongo kingdom (Mani kongo).

masquerade A festival in which masks and costumes are worn. many African cultures have elaborate masquerades marking important RITES OF PASSAGE such as initiation.

mbira (thumb piano, lamellaphone, sanza) An instrument widely used in sub-Saharan Africa. It is made of tuned metal strips attached to a resonating chamber (often a hollowed-out gourd). The keys are plucked with the thumbs.

mestico A Portuguese term used in Angola to denote a person of mixed European and African descent.

mganda A warlike dance performed by the Tonga of Zambia.

Mobandi A seasonal ritual of the Mbenga, in which they beat themselves with branches to dispel evil spirits.

Mukanda A male initiation ceremony of the Chokwe and other peoples.

mulopwe A ruler of the former Luba kingdom. The mulopwe reigned with divine authority, and was thought to have supernatural powers.

mwaash a mbooy Masks that were formerly used by Kuba rulers as tools of royal justice. The masks were made of wood and cowrie shells, and the wearer was supposed to be able to assess a person's guilt or innocence.

mwata yamvo Title of the ruler of the former Lunda empire.

negritude (French: "blackness") A literary movement founded in the 1930s by West African and Caribbean expatriates in France. Its aims were to celebrate African culture and oppose colonial rule.

ngil A society that existed among communities of the Fang people in precolonial times. Its members had political and judicial power, and often punished or executed people found guilty of witchcraft. It was widely feared and respected by the Fang, but was disbanded by the authorities of French Equatorial Africa in the early 20th century.

nkisi nkondi "Power figures" made by the Kongo people; they are stabbed with iron blades or nails in DIVINATION ceremonies to rouse the figures' magical or medicinal properties.

pastoralist A person who lives by herding livestock such as cattle or sheep and generally pursues a nomadic or seminomadic lifestyle.

polygyny The practice of marrying more than one wife.

protectorate A state or territory under the control of a stronger foreign nation. The term was often used by European powers to refer to their African colonies.

raffia cloth A textile made from the young leaves of the raffia palm tree. Once commonly employed for clothing in the Congo Basin it was also used for currency in precolonial times, being cut into squares called *mbongo*.

rainforest Dense forest that grows in tropical zones with abundant rainfall all year round. The trees are nearly all broadleaved evergreen species, such as ironwood and mahogany. The temperature is around 27°F (80°C) throughout the year, with eighty-percent humidity. Growth is rapid and lush. Rainforests are rich in plants and animals (containing half of all the world's species).

reliquary (adj. and noun) A container used to hold the remains of a person, or a term to describe such a vessel. Reliquary figures used by the Fang were known as BIERI.

rite of passage A ceremony, such as initiation into adulthood or marriage, that marks the passage of a person from one stage of life to another.

rubbing oracle A means of divination used by several African peoples. A diviner rubs an item such as a carved piece of wood or stone across a wooden board and poses questions, asking for example who might be responsible for bewitching another person. When the rubbed item seems to move more (or less) freely, this is taken to be a positive (or negative) answer.

savanna Tropical grassland dominated by various species of perennial grasses interspersed with varying numbers of shrubs and low trees.

shantytown An area of impermanent housing, usually made from scrap materials, on the outskirts of large cities where poor migrants to urban areas live. Shantytowns often lack running water, drainage, and other basic amenities.

shifting cultivation A farming method (once termed "slash-and-burn" agriculture) that involves clearing an area of forest for temporary crop growing. After harvesting the crop, the farmers move on to a new location. This farming method is widely practiced in the forest regions of Central Africa.

shongo A throwing knife equipped with multiple blades. A deadly weapon, the shongo spun through the air when thrown, which enabled it to inflict maximum damage on its target. In Central Africa, the Azande and the Kuba were renowned for their skill in using the shongo.

subsistence farming A type of agriculture in which all the crops grown are eaten by the farmer and his or her family, leaving nothing to sell for profit ("cash crops") at market.

taboo A restriction or prohibition in a culture, established by convention, which prevents a person from acting in ways seen as inappropriate. Many taboos relate to tasks that must not be undertaken by one sex or the other, food that must not be eaten, or certain forms of clothing that may not be worn.

talking drum A drum formerly widely used by some African peoples to communicate between and within villages. The pitch of the talking drum can be altered to mimic the tonal qualities of African languages; often secret messages whose cipher was known only to senior men would be encoded in the beats.

tsetse fly An insect that carries parasites that transmit disease to both people and cattle. It is widespread in East and Central Africa, and is responsible for the spread of sleeping sickness (trypanosomasis). In Bantu, the word *tsetse* literally means "the fly that kills."

Umutomboko A celebration held by the Lunda of Zambia, commemorating the migration of their ancestors from the north and their military prowess.

urbanization The process by which a rural area becomes more built-up and industrialized. This generally involves the migration of rural people into cities.

wattle-and-daub A building technique that uses clay or adobe plastered on a latticework made of sticks.

yanda A carved wooden statuette used in the Zande religion to protect members of the MANI society from harm.

General books:

Beckwith, C., and Fisher, A. *African Ceremonies* (Harry N. Abrams, Inc., New York, NY, 2002).

Hynson, C. *Exploration of Africa* (Barrons Juveniles, Hauppauge, NY, 1998).

Mitchell, P. J. *African Connections: Archaeological Perspectives on Africa and the Wider World* (AltaMira Press, Walnut Creek, CA, 2005).

Morris, P., Barrett, A., Murray, A., and Smits van Oyen, M. *Wild Africa* (BBC, London, UK, 2001).

Murray, J. *Africa: Cultural Atlas for Young People* (Facts On File, New York, NY, 2003).

Philips, T. (ed.) *Africa: The Art of a Continent* (Prestel, Munich, Germany, 1995).

Rasmussen, R. K. *Modern African Political Leaders* (Facts On File, New York, NY, 1998).

Reader, J. *Africa: A Biography of the Continent* (Penguin, New York, NY, 1998).

Sheehan, S. *Great African Kingdoms* (Raintree/Steck-Vaughn, Austin, TX, 1998).

Stuart, C., and Stuart, T. *Africa—A Natural History* (Swan Hill Press, Shrewsbury, UK, 1995).

Temko, F. *Traditional Crafts from Africa* (Lerner Publishing, Minneapolis, MN, 1996).

The Diagram Group *Encyclopedia of African Peoples* (Facts On File, New York, NY, 2000).

The Diagram Group *Encyclopedia of African Nations and Civilizations* (Facts On File, New York, NY, 2003).

Thomas, V. M. *Lest We Forget: The Passage from Africa to Slavery and Emancipation* (Crown Publishers, New York, NY, 1997).

Books specific to this volume:

Jordan, M. *The Kongo Kingdom* (Franklin Watts, Danbury, CT, 1999).

Lyman, F. *Inside the Dzanga-Sangha Rain Forest: Exploring the Heart of Central Africa* (Workman Publishing, New York, NY, 1998).

Schildkrout, E., and Keim, C. A. *African Reflections: Art from Northeastern Zaïre* (American Museum of Natural History, New York, NY, 1990).

Struhsaker, T. T. *Ecology of an African Rainforest* (University of Florida Press, Gainesville, FL, 1999).

The Diagram Group *History of East Africa* (Facts On File, New York, NY, 2003).

Turnbull, C. *The Forest People* (Touchstone Books, Carmichael, CA, 1987)

Vansina, J. *Paths in the Rainforests: Towards a History of Political Tradition in Equatorial Africa* (University of Wisconsin Press, Madison, WI, 1990).

Useful Web sites:

www.bioko.org
Focus on the island of Bioko, Equatorial Guinea.

www.congo2005.be
Cultures and history of Congo (DRC) from Belgium's Royal Museum of Central Africa.

dpls.dacc.wisc.edu/slavedata/index.html
Data on the transatlantic slave trade.

www.gabonnationalparks.com
Web site on ongoing wildlife and ecology conservation programs in Gabon.

www.ggcg.st
Biodiversity of the islands of the Gulf of Guinea.

www.nationalgeographic.com/congotrek
One man's celebrated trek through the rainforest.

www.pygmies.info
Web site on the Baka rainforest people.

www.rainforestweb.org/Rainforest_Regions/Africa
Resources on rainforest conservation and related issues.

www.zamnet.zm
Resources on Zambia.

www.smpl.org

ISMP0014838996